Mahomtt

Marmarica

Bermu

Ammon

AEGYPTVS

Syene

Cayrū

Nilus fl.

Medina

ARABIA Petrea

ARABIA Fe

Mare Rubrū

SYAE
fertum

Sawied

NVBIAE
Regnum

Nubis

Meroe

REGNVM
Orgueng

PIA

REGNVM
Habesih

Monoculi

Hamarich
Sedes Prę
te Iohan

REGNV
de Seyl

REGNVM
Melinde

Azania regio

Tellus Psi
tacorum

QVIOLA
Regnum

Zapnala
aurifodina

AFRICÆ
extremitas

Capur bone spei

Ptolemy's map of Africa, from *Ptolemy Geographica Universalis,* known as the Muenster edition, published in 1545. Reproduced by courtesy of the British Library Board.

An Atlas of African History

J. D. FAGE

AFRICANA PUBLISHING COMPANY
A division of Holmes & Meier Publishers, Inc.
New York

Second edition first published in the
United States of America 1978 by
AFRICANA PUBLISHING COMPANY
A division of Holmes & Meier Publishers, Inc.
30 Irving Place, New York, N.Y. 10003

Second edition copyright © 1978 by J. D. Fage

Library of Congress Cataloging in Publication Data
Fage, J D
  An atlas of African history.

  Includes index.
  1. Africa—Historical geography—Maps. I. Title.
G2446.S1F3 1978   911'.6   78–16131
ISBN 0–8419–0429–4
ISBN 0–8419–0430–8 pbk.

PRINTED IN GREAT BRITAIN

Foreword

When this *Atlas of African History* was first published in 1958, practically the whole continent was still under colonial rule, and the academic study of its peoples' past was only just beginning. Nearly twenty years later, the situation is very different. There is hardly an African territory which is not now recognised as an independent state. But this momentous change need not have occasioned a completely new edition of the *Atlas*. As in fact was done in 1963 and 1965, it could have been dealt with simply by the revision of those maps showing recent political history. What has necessitated the production of a wholly revised second edition has been the rapid and expansive flowering since the mid-1950s of historical and archaeological research into the African past. This is directly associated with the growth of universities, as of education generally, in the new Africa, and of the acceptance of the history and archaeology of Africa as valid subjects for study in the universities of other countries. If only because the colonial period of African history was so very short—for the most part concentrated within the years 1880–1960, hardly more than a human life-span—many of the most spectacular advances in knowledge have related to the very much longer period of some two thousand years since iron-working was initiated south of the Sahara, and particularly perhaps to the seven or so centuries before the Europeans' scramble for African colonies, the period during which most of the polities they conquered were shaped. As a result, many of the maps originally conceived for this formative period of African history had become inadequate or unsatisfactory, and it also became possible to conceive new maps relating to times or to areas whose history had hitherto been chiefly characterised by its obscurity. Thus, comparing the *Atlas* now presented to the public with the original edition of 1958, there are 21 completely new maps, while 11 of the old ones have been deleted, and quite a few of the others have been subjected to some alteration or rearrangement.

The great growth in African historical and archaeological research in the last quarter of a century has also had the apparently paradoxical consequence that it is now impracticable to provide a list of acknowledgements of the kind that was given in the first edition, and which was in effect a guide to the sources for the *Atlas*. When in the 1950s I was first working on the idea of a historical atlas for Africa, it was necessary to hunt out reliable—or seemingly reliable—information for it from a strange variety of sources, not all of which were overtly historical in intent. There were no major histories of the continent, or of substantial parts of it, which one could rely upon for general guidance, and

there was no great corpus of scholarly historical monographs or journal articles to which one could refer for authoritative assessment of points of detail. Today these things exist in relative abundance, and an accurate list of all the scholars and their works I have drawn from—unconsciously as well as consciously—would be impossibly lengthy. (There are, however, a number of maps in the new edition which draw directly on other people's work or which deliberately reflect their own specialist judgements; here acknowledgements are provided in the appropriate places.)

Much of my own knowledge of African history today comes from my good fortune in being associated with Professor Roland Oliver in the planning and direction of two major enterprises, *The Journal of African History*, which the Cambridge University Press began to publish in 1960, and the *Cambridge History of Africa*, in eight volumes, which began to come from the same publishers in 1975. Such ventures are symptomatic of the new maturity of African historical studies, and it is to these and their counterparts produced by other editors and publishers that the student should turn if he wants to explore the sources now available for the elucidation of the history of African peoples and of its spatial dimensions. The general histories almost invariably provide excellent bibliographies. In addition to the *Cambridge History* already mentioned, UNESCO is sponsoring a *General History of Africa* on the same scale (also in eight volumes, each edited by a different African scholar); and one might also mention the *Histoire Générale de l'Afrique Noire*, another major cooperative effort, albeit in only two volumes, edited by Hubert Deschamps (Presses Universitaires de France, 1970–71). There are also some important cooperative regional histories, for example the *History of West Africa* edited by J. F. Ade Ajayi and Michael Crowder (2 vols, Longmans, 1971–4), *The History of East Africa* in three volumes, each with its own editors, published by the Clarendon Press (1963–75), and *The Oxford History of South Africa* edited by Monica Wilson and Leonard Thompson (2 vols, Clarendon Press, 1969–71). Nor are these the only major works of synthesis: other examples—and English language examples only—are A. G. Hopkins's *An Economic History of West Africa* (2nd edition, Longmans, 1975); the essays on *Pre-Colonial African Trade* edited by Richard Gray and David Birmingham (Oxford, 1970) or on *African Societies in Southern Africa* edited by Leonard Thompson (Heinemann, 1969); or—on the archaeological front—such a book as Brian M. Fagan's *Southern Africa during the Iron Age* (Thames and Hudson, 1965).

The importance of the specialist journals also cannot be too much stressed, and not only for the minutiae of African history. Important sections of this history are only being disclosed through current research, and ongoing research may also challenge accepted interpretations of apparently better-known history. Indeed it may not unusually change the 'facts' on which these interpretations have been based. There can also often be an appreciable time-lag before the results of research published in the journals find their way into the major works of synthesis. Nothing approaching a complete listing of these journals can be attempted here but, to name only English language publications, the *International Journal of African Historical Studies* (Boston, 1968–) and *History in Africa* (Brandeis University, 1974–) have achieved much the same kind of international standing as the pioneering *Journal of African History*; and one should not neglect more local journals, such as *The Transactions of the Historical Society of Ghana* (Legon, 1952–), *The Journal of the Historical Society of Nigeria* (Ibadan, 1956–), *Azania* (British Institute of History and Archaeology in Eastern Africa, Nairobi, 1966–) or *The West African Journal of Archaeology* (Ibadan, 1971–).

In the Foreword to the original 1958 edition of the *Atlas*, it seemed necessary to offer a number of explanations as to what might or might not be attempted in an atlas of African history. The fact that the public has never since allowed the *Atlas* to go out of print, together with the changes made for this new edition, would seem to make most of these superfluous in 1977. But there is one point which is still as valid as it was when first made in 1958. I then wrote:

> It has not seemed practicable to attempt throughout the *Atlas* to standardise the spelling of geographical and proper names. Nor perhaps would this be desirable, for notwithstanding the fact that there are now generally accepted rules for the transliteration of names from African languages and from Arabic, it should be remembered that these names have passed into history and into English usage at various times and in a variety of ways, often proceeding through the medium of one or more other languages on the way. The form of a name which may be most appropriate for a student requiring information about a particular part of Africa at a time when it was, let us say, under Muslim or Portuguese control, may not

therefore be the form most appropriate to a map of the same area dealing with the earlier history of its peoples. Again, this form may well differ from that which has become standardised on modern topographical maps as a result of the work of nineteenth century European explorers, or of administrators to whom consistency has seemed more important than the rules of transliteration now recommended by linguistic authorities. A note on some of the more general difficulties with regard to Bantu and Arabic names is prefixed to the Index, and some attempt has been made to indicate variant or alternative names in the Index itself.

It may indeed be said that the problem has been compounded since 1958, for one result of independence has been that the new African states have naturally tended to replace overtly colonial topographical names, especially those celebrating European pioneers or propagandists of empire, with more appropriate African ones. A list of some of the more significant of these changes has therefore been provided in an Appendix. (It must, however, be appreciated that it has always been the case that the English or other foreign names for a town or geographical feature in another country may not be the same as the names used by the local people: thus Morocco and Egypt are the accepted English names for countries which their own people call al-Mamlakah al-Maghribiya and Misr respectively. It is possible, therefore, that common European usage may retain some of the longer established European topographical names in Africa.)

In 1958, I acknowledged my gratitude to Maureen Verity, 'who has accomplished the formidable task of interpreting sketches of my intentions and transmitting them into finished maps with the grace and clarity to which the following pages bear witness'. I am glad to say that she has been available to draw the new maps, and also that her contribution to the achievement of the *Atlas* is now marked by adding her name to mine on the title page.

Finally, I would like to record that I dedicated the original edition of the *Atlas* to two great teachers of history whose influence undoubtedly did much to inspire me to follow in their footsteps. Alas, both are now dead, and initials will no longer suffice. The new edition is therefore offered *In Memoriam* Tom Stavely, 1893–1962, and Frank Reyner Salter, 1887–1967.

J.D.F.

Contents

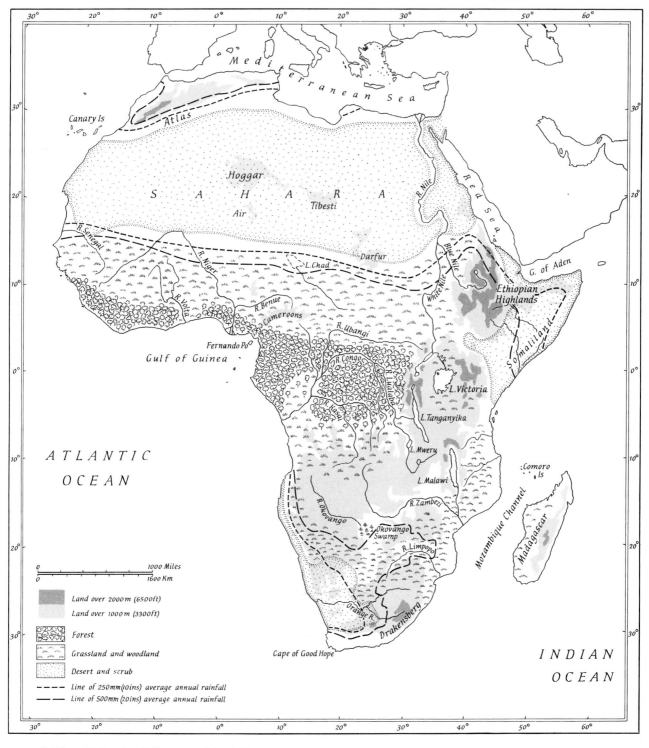

**1 Africa: Principal Geographical Features,
Rainfall and Vegetation**

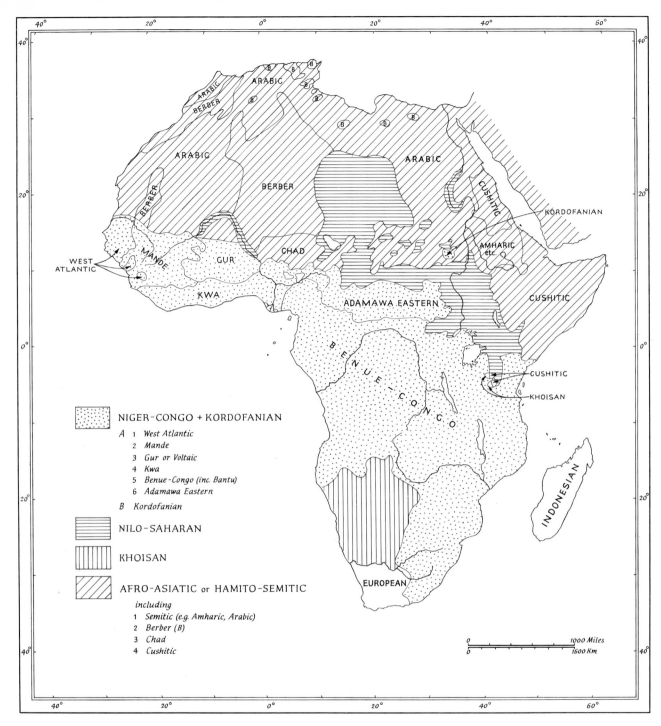

2 Language Families of Africa

This map is based on material in J. H. Greenberg, *The Languages of Africa* (2nd edition, Mouton, 1966).

Map labels:

NIGER-CONGO + KORDOFANIAN

A 1 *West Atlantic*
2 *Mande*
3 *Gur or Voltaic*
4 *Kwa*
5 *Benue-Congo (inc. Bantu)*
6 *Adamawa Eastern*

B *Kordofanian*

NILO-SAHARAN

KHOISAN

AFRO-ASIATIC or HAMITO-SEMITIC

including
1 *Semitic (e.g. Amharic, Arabic)*
2 *Berber (B)*
3 *Chad*
4 *Cushitic*

0 — 1000 Miles
0 — 1600 Km

ARABIC · BERBER · CUSHITIC · KORDOFANIAN · AMHARIC etc. · WEST ATLANTIC · MANDE · GUR · CHAD · KWA · ADAMAWA EASTERN · BENUE-CONGO · KHOISAN · INDONESIAN · EUROPEAN

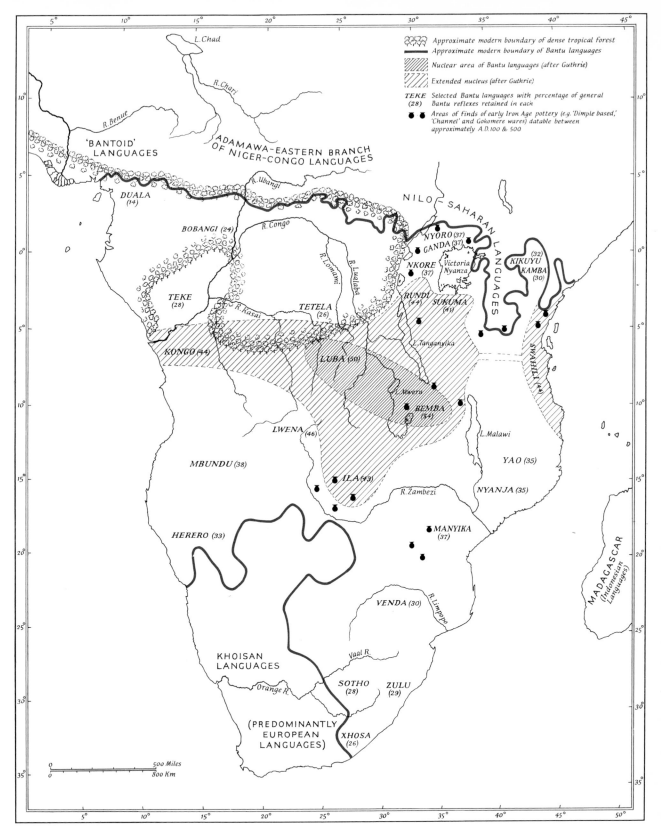

3 The Peopling of the Southern Half of Africa

This map incorporates data established by Malcolm Guthrie in his
*Comparative Bantu: An Introduction to the Comparative Linguistics
and Pre-History of the Bantu Languages* (4 vols, Gregg International
Publishers, 1967–71).

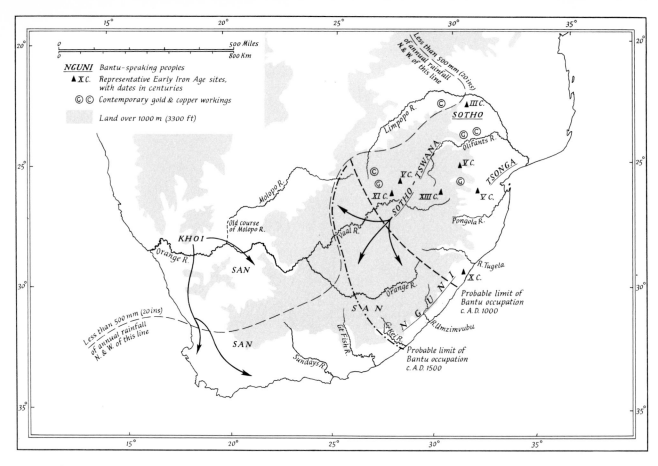

4   The Peopling of Southern Africa

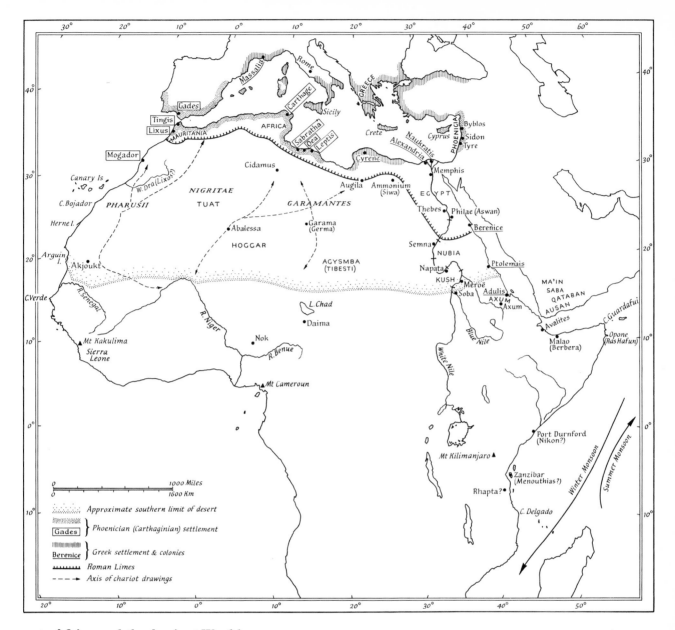

5 Africa and the Ancient World

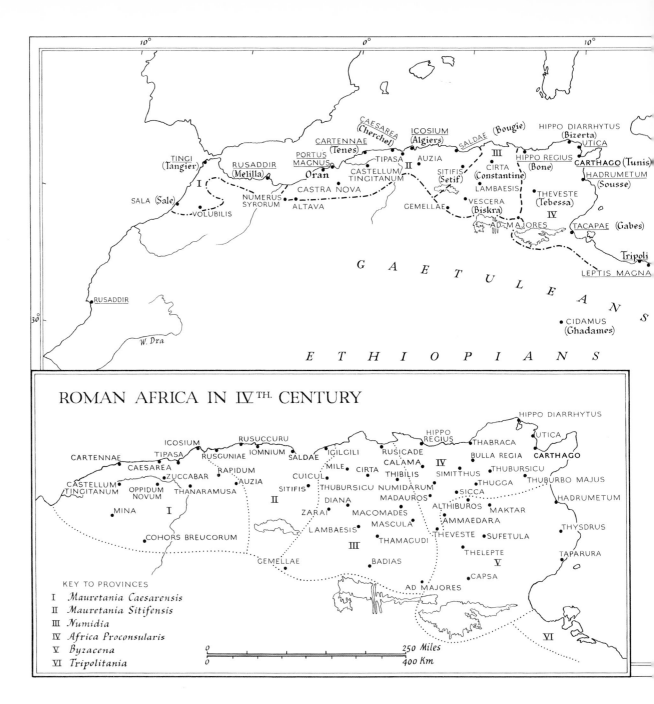

ROMAN AFRICA IN IVᵀᴴ CENTURY

KEY TO PROVINCES
I   *Mauretania Caesarensis*
II *Mauretania Sitifensis*
III *Numidia*
IV *Africa Proconsularis*
V   *Byzacena*
VI *Tripolitania*

0 _____ 250 Miles
0 _____ 400 Km

6 Roman Africa

The main map shows the greatest extent of Roman dominion in Africa, in the middle of the third century A.D., with the major administrative divisions at that time. Note that to the Romans the word *Africa* was properly applied only to one province, though in a more general sense it could mean North Africa with the exception of Egypt. The territory south of the area of Roman control was generally referred to as *Ethiopia*, though in a more specific sense Ethiopia was the Nile valley above Egypt, *Ethiopia supra Aegyptum*.

Roman settlement was densest in the provinces of Africa and Numidia, and in the inset map an attempt has been made to show, as well as the reorganisation of provinces which took place at the end of the third century, the large number of Roman towns in this region. To the west of Numidia, the Berber tribes effectively confined Roman settlement to the narrow coastal plain, and it was hardly more extensive than the area earlier dominated by the Carthaginian trading posts (underlined on the map). Between Africa proper and Egypt, except in Cyrenaica (initially colonised by Greeks), the desert presses close to the sea, and once again Roman settlement was confined to coastal towns. In Egypt the Nile valley was held as far south as the First Cataract at Aswan, the Dodekaschinus being held as a buffer

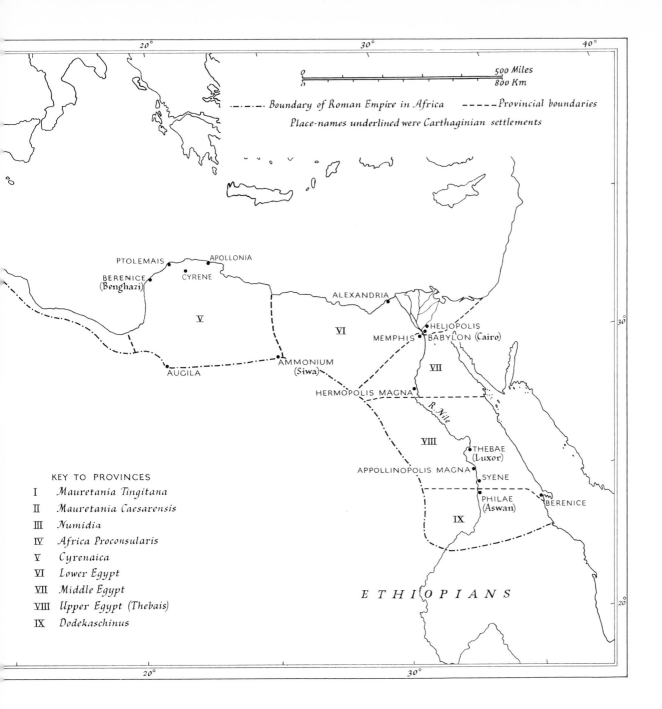

0   500 Miles
0   800 Km

—·—·— *Boundary of Roman Empire in Africa*   ----- *Provincial boundaries*

Place-names underlined were Carthaginian settlements

PTOLEMAIS   APOLLONIA

BERENICE   CYRENE
(Benghazi)

ALEXANDRIA

V

HELIOPOLIS
MEMPHIS · BABYLON (Cairo)

VI

AMMONIUM
AUGILA   (Siwa)

VII

HERMOPOLIS MAGNA

R. Nile

VIII

THEBAE
(Luxor)

APPOLLINOPOLIS MAGNA
SYENE

PHILAE
(Aswan)   BERENICE

IX

E T H I O P I A N S

KEY TO PROVINCES
I   *Mauretania Tingitana*
II   *Mauretania Caesarensis*
III   *Numidia*
IV   *Africa Proconsularis*
V   *Cyrenaica*
VI   *Lower Egypt*
VII   *Middle Egypt*
VIII   *Upper Egypt (Thebais)*
IX   *Dodekaschinus*

province against the attacks of the Nobatae, to whom it was lost at the end of the third century.

The inset shows the provinces of the reduced empire in north-western Africa of the fourth century A.D., together with the sites of some of the more important Roman settlements. It will be seen that the fertile plains of modern Tunisia and eastern Algeria were the scene of intensive colonisation. The area effectively controlled by the Byzantine emperors after the reconquest from the Vandals was limited to this zone of intensive settlement, and did not include Mauretania Caesarensis, the western part of Mauretania Sitifensis, and the southern part of Tripolitania.

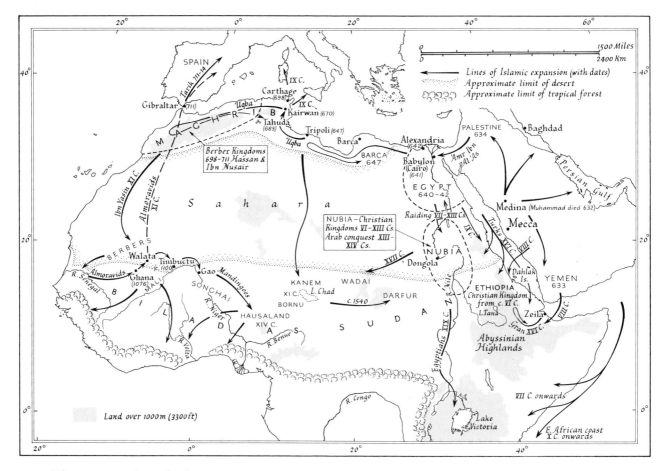

7   The Penetration of Islam

The introduction of Islam into northern Africa is synonymous with the Arab conquest, though in Egypt something like three centuries elapsed before Islam had generally replaced Christianity as the religion of the conquered people, and in north-western Africa Islamisation did not begin to be complete until after the invasion and settlement of Beduin tribes in the eleventh century (see Map 13). The penetration of Islam across the Sahara was in part the work of Arab nomads, but was chiefly a consequence of the development of trans-Saharan trade (see Map 11), itself largely a consequence of the adoption of the camel by the people of North Africa, a process which was complete by about the fourth century A.D. The expansion of Islam in the Sudan, other than in the Nilotic Sudan, where it was due to the Arab conquest of Christian kingdoms, was largely carried out by Islamised peoples native to the Sudan, e.g., Mande traders and state-builders and Hausa traders. In the eleventh century an Islamic movement originating in the western Sahara, that of the Almoravids (*al-Murabitun*), is carried northwards to the conquest of Morocco and Spain (Map 13).

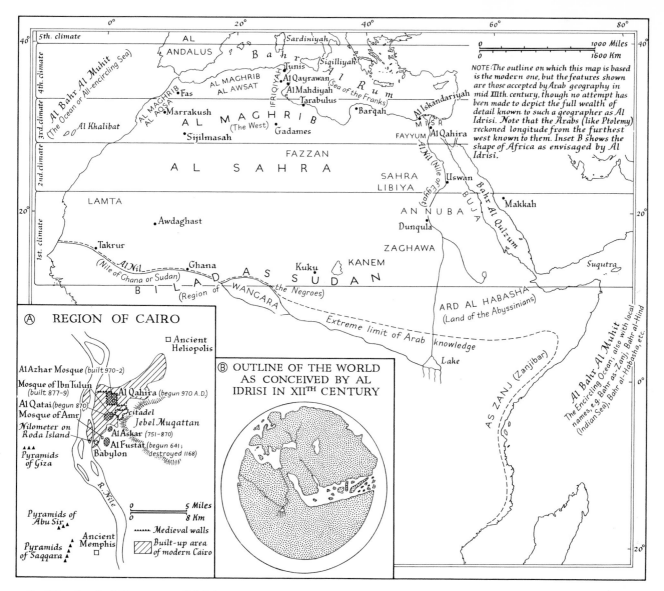

8 The Arabs' Concept of Africa

The map shows the following labelled features:

Scale: 0 — 1000 Miles, 0 — 1600 Km

NOTE: The outline on which this map is based is the modern one, but the features shown are those accepted by Arab geography in mid XIIIth. century, though no attempt has been made to depict the full wealth of detail known to such a geographer as Al Idrisi. Note that the Arabs (like Ptolemy) reckoned longitude from the furthest west known to them. Inset B shows the shape of Africa as envisaged by Al Idrisi.

5th. climate
4th. climate
3rd. climate
2nd. climate
1st. climate

AL ANDALUS
Al Bahr Al Muhit (The Ocean or All-encircling Sea)
Bahr Al Rum (Sea of the Franks)
Sardiniyah
Siqilliyah
Tunis
Al Qayrawan
Al Mahdiyah
Tarabulus
IFRIQIYAH
Barqah
Al Iskandariyah
MISR
FAYYUM
Al Qahira
Fas
AL MAGHRIB AL AWSAT
AL MAGHRIB AL AQSA
Marrakush
AL MAGHRIB (The West)
Al Khalibat
Sijilmasah
Gadames
FAZZAN
AL SAHRA
SAHRA LIBIYA
Uswan
Al Nil (Nile of Egypt)
Bahr Al Quizum
BUJA
Makkah
LAMTA
Awdaghast
AN NUBA
Dunqula
Takrur
ZAGHAWA
Al Nil (Nile of Ghana or Sudan)
Ghana
Kuku
KANEM
AS SUDAN
BILAD (Region of WANGARA) (the Negroes)
ARD AL HABASHA (Land of the Abyssinians)
Extreme limit of Arab knowledge
Lake
Suqutra
AS ZANJ (Zanjibar)
Al Bahr Al Muhit — The Encircling Ocean; also with local names, e.g. Bahr as-Zanj; Bahr al-Hind (Indian Sea), Bahr al-Habasha, etc.

(A) **REGION OF CAIRO**

☐ Ancient Heliopolis
Al Azhar Mosque (built 970-2)
Mosque of Ibn Tulun (built 877-9)
Al Qatai (begun 870)
Mosque of Amr
Nilometer on Roda Island
Al Qahira (begun 970 A.D.)
citadel
Jebel Muqattan
Al Askar (751-870)
Al Fustat (begun 641; destroyed 1168)
Babylon
▲▲▲ Pyramids of Giza
R. Nile
0 — 5 Miles
0 — 8 Km
▲▲ Pyramids of Abu Sir
Pyramids of Saqqara
☐ Ancient Memphis
···· Medieval walls
▨ Built-up area of modern Cairo

(B) **OUTLINE OF THE WORLD AS CONCEIVED BY AL IDRISI IN XIITH CENTURY**

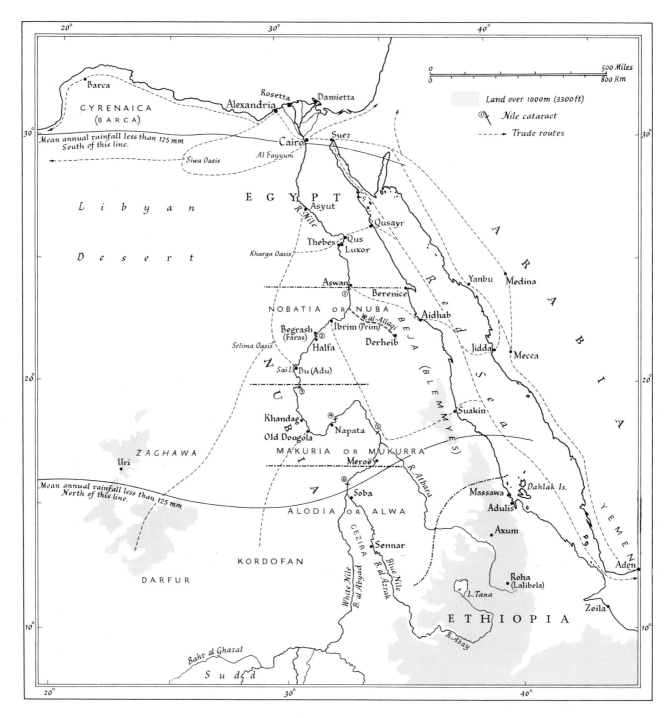

9 The Nile Valley, VIth to XIVth Centuries

The ancient kingdom of Kush, with its centre first at Napata and then at Meroë, which had preserved in the Nile Valley between Egypt and the Abyssinian highlands its own brand of Egyptian-derived civilisation during many centuries in which Egypt itself was under foreign domination (Assyrians, Persians, Greeks, Romans), ultimately disappeared in IVth century A.D., the final blow being the sack of Meroë by Ezana (c. A.D. 320–50), the first Christian king of Axum. The inheritance of Kush then passed to the three Nubian kingdoms shown on this map, in all of which during the course of the VIth century Christianity was adopted as the official religion. By the time of the Arab conquest of Egypt (A.D. 641),

the two northern kingdoms had united into the single kingdom of Dongola, which was not finally to go under to the Arabs and to Islam until XIVth century (see Map 7). Meanwhile Arab control of the Levant and of the Red Sea had meant the disruption of the Red Sea trade of the Greek merchants and of the east–west trade between the Yemen and the Nile Valley which had together formed the basis of the prosperity and power of Axum, and its Christian monarchy accordingly withdrew from the Red Sea coastland of Eritrea into the highlands of Abyssinia, where it ultimately developed into the Christian kingdom of Ethiopia (see Map 21).

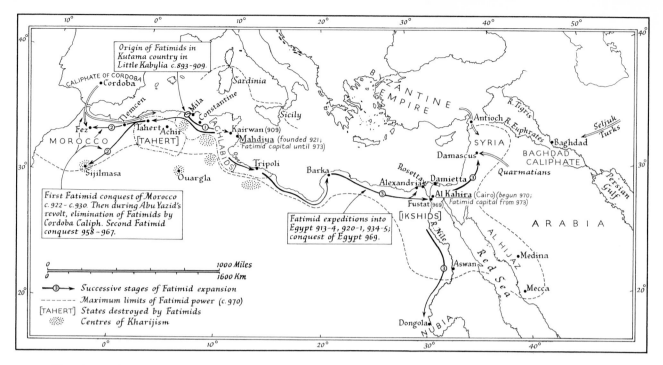

Map legend and annotations:

Origin of Fatimids in Kutama country in Little Kabylia c. 893–909.

First Fatimid conquest of Morocco c. 922 – c. 930. Then during Abu Yazid's revolt, elimination of Fatimids by Cordoba Caliph. Second Fatimid conquest 958 – 967.

Fatimid expeditions into Egypt 913-4, 920-1, 934-5; conquest of Egypt 969.

Al Kahira (Cairo) (begun 970; Fatimid capital from 973)

Mahdiya (founded 921; Fatimid capital until 973)

───③─→ Successive stages of Fatimid expansion
- - - - - Maximum limits of Fatimid power (c. 970)
[TAHERT] States destroyed by Fatimids
∴∴∴ Centres of Kharijism

10 Northern Africa during the Fatimid Epoch, Xth Century

After the Arab conquest under Hassan and Ibn Nusair (Map 7), the Maghrib did not long remain under Caliphal control. In Ifriqiya (the Arabic equivalent of the Roman Africa, i.e. modern Tunisia), the Aghlabid governors, who conquered Sicily and Sardinia, soon became virtually independent of the Caliphate, while in the west and centre Arab dynasties, such as the Idrisids, and Berber states, such as Tahert, arose which found expression for local particularism in the espousal of schismatic Muslim movements, such as Shi'ism or the quasi-republican Kharijism, which involved rejection of the orthodox Abbasid Caliphate. The (Shi'ite)

Fatimids, and their champions, the Kutama Berbers from Little Kabylia, conquered Ifriqiya during 902–909 and established an independent Caliphate. The Fatimid Caliphs, though until 946 themselves seriously threatened by Kharijist inspired revolt in Ifriqiya, sought to challenge the Abbasids in Egypt and also to assert their authority over the rest of the Maghrib. With the help of the Sanhaja dynasty of the Zirids of Achir, the western Maghrib was eventually reduced to obedience (958–67), and with their rear secured, the Fatimids were then able to establish themselves in Egypt (969) and to conquer Syria from the Abbasids.

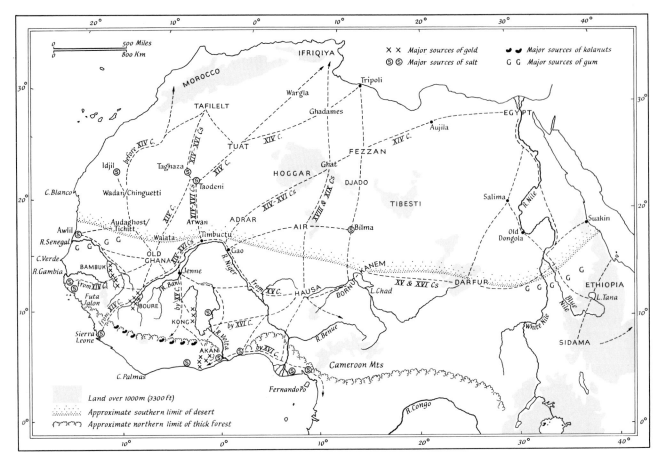

II   Trade Routes of Northern Africa, Xth to XVIIIth Centuries

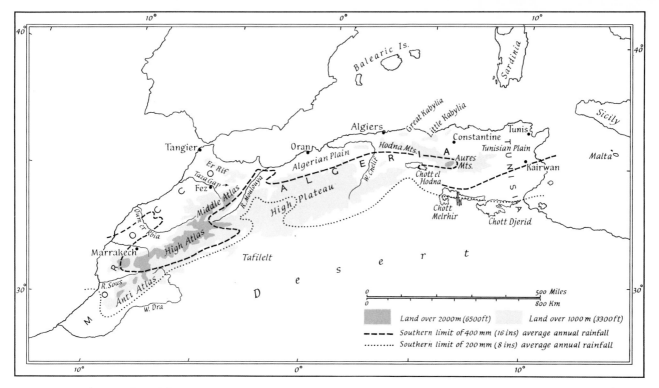

12 The Geographical Setting for the History of the Maghrib

The Maghrib is in effect an island between Africa and Europe, an island more easily accessible by sea from Europe across the Mediterranean narrows and islands than it is from the rest of Africa, from which it is separated by wide stretches of desert. Its history has thus been more Mediterranean than African: it has often been dominated by European civilisations (Maps 6, 19, 51), and on one important occasion it provided a bridge across which a culture originating in Asia, Islam, was transported into Europe, principally by North African Berbers.

Geography divides the Maghrib into three parts, two ends and a centre. In the east is the modern Tunisia, the Africa of Roman colonisation (Map 6), possessing the only extensive area of flat and relatively fertile land, even if the southern half of the country, the Byzacena of the Romans, is not agriculturally very productive without artificial irrigation. Historically Tunisia has served as the Maghribian base of developed and stable civilisations. On the other hand, Morocco, the far west, a land of high mountain ranges separating narrow plains which are linked only along the coast, has always tended to be the stronghold of North African Berber resistance to

change and to alien rule, whether of Romans, Arabs, Turks, or Europeans.

What since the XIXth century has become known as Algeria is a region of transition, which in the Kabyles and Aures affords mountain strongholds of resistance comparable to those of Morocco, while its coastal plain offers opportunities for agriculture comparable to those of Tunisia. However, the plain is open to raids from the pastoral nomads of the high steppe plateau, who are naturally hostile to control by sedentary peoples. Historically Algeria has tended to be a region in which the rulers of Tunisia have competed with those of Morocco for control, though neither have usually succeeded in controlling it for long. Indeed, control of the whole length of the Maghrib by a power based on one of its ends has rarely proved practicable, with the result that the middle, Algerian, region has often lapsed into a state of anarchy or near anarchy characterised by the conflict between the nomads of the steppes and the rulers of the plain. In the XIXth century it was this weakness at the centre which afforded the opportunity for the entry of the French and their eventual mastery of the whole Maghrib.

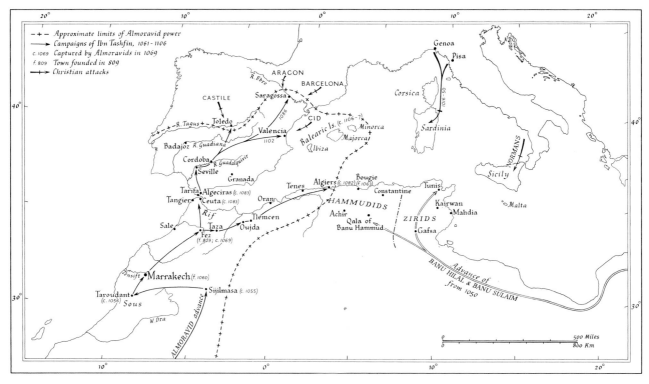

13 The Empire of the Almoravids, A.D. *c.*1050–
*c.*1140 (see opposite)

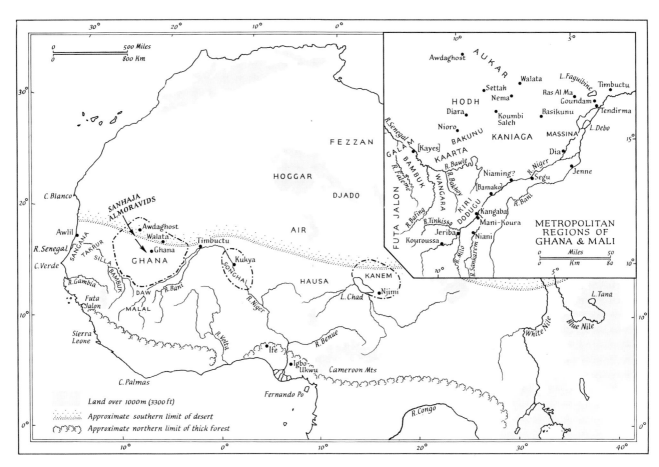

14 The Sudan in the XIth Century

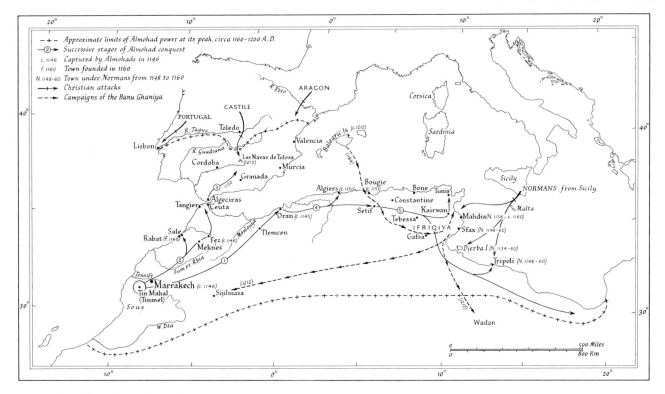

- – + – Approximate limits of Almohad power at its peak, circa 1160–1200 A.D.
- –②→ Successive stages of Almohad conquest
- c.1146 Captured by Almohads in 1146
- f.1160 Town founded in 1160
- N.1148–60 Town under Normans from 1148 to 1160
- →+→ Christian attacks
- – – – Campaigns of the Banu Ghaniya

15   The Empire of the Almohads, A.D. *c.* 1140–*c*.1250

The formalisation of Almoravid government pro-voked hostility from the Masmuda tribes of the Moroccan Atlas and the Zanata of the western steppes. These welcomed the preaching of Ibn Tu-mart that the Almoravids had no monopoly claim to righteousness, rose against them as the Almohads (*al-Muwahhidum,* 'the monotheists'), and quickly established their dominion throughout Morocco. The Almohads were soon called into Spain, where Christian princes were advancing in the time of Almoravid decline. They also moved into the eastern Maghrib to repel the Normans and to try to control the Beduin. The result was the establishment of an Almohad dominion over all western Islam.

13   The Empire of the Almoravids, A.D. *c.*1050–*c*.1140

When in 973 the Fatimids (Map 10) transferred their capital to Egypt, they entrusted Ifriqiya to the gover-norship of the Zirids, and as a result these lost con-trol of their own homeland to their Hammudid kinsmen. In the west, the Zanata pastoral nomads became the dominant force until their power was de-stroyed by the Almoravids (*al-Murabitun,* 'people of the ribat'), a coalition of Sanhaja desert tribes under the inspiration of a puritanical Islam, who rapidly established a major empire over the western Mag-hrib and Muslim Spain, with its capital at Mar-rakech. After the Zirids declared their independence of the Fatimids by acknowledging the Abbasid Caliph, they had to face invasion from Beduin Arab tribes arriving from Egypt, first and foremost the Banu Hilal and Banu Sulaim. The result was a great weakening of organised government in the eastern Maghrib outside the coastal towns, and this facili-tated the attacks of the Normans from Sicily that are shown on Map 15.

16 The Mamluk Empire at its Greatest Extent,
A.D. **1260–1340**

After the decline of the Fatimid power and the collapse of their empire, Egypt passed into the hands of Saladin (1169–93), a Kurdish general from Syria, whose main aim was to build up a strong Muslim power in Egypt and Syria to oppose the Crusaders. His work was con-

tinued and the Christians finally expelled, by the Bahri Mamluk Sultans, Baybars (1260–77), and Kalacun (1279–90) and his descendants, who also succeeded in repelling the westward advance of the Il Khan Mongols.

17 The States of the Maghrib, XIIIth and XIVth Centuries

A power so extended over a difficult terrain as that of the Almohads was difficult to defend, and by the end of the XIIth century the Almohads were facing attack on three fronts. To deal with the attacks of the Banu Ghaniya (see Map 15), the Almoravids placed Ifriqiya under the viceregal government of the Hafsid family. This became independent as the Almohad regime was weakened by its failure to stem renewed Christian ad-

vances in Spain, which was all but lost to Islam following the battle of Las Navas de Tolosa in 1212 (Map 15), or to control the Beduin who were now active in their Moroccan homeland. Ultimately power passed in the central Maghrib and in Morocco to two Zanata groups, the 'Abd al-Wahids and the Merinids respectively.

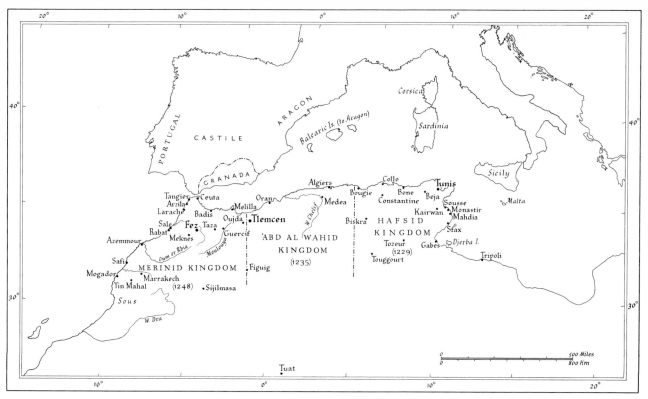

17 The States of the Maghrib, XIIIth and XIVth Centuries (see opposite)

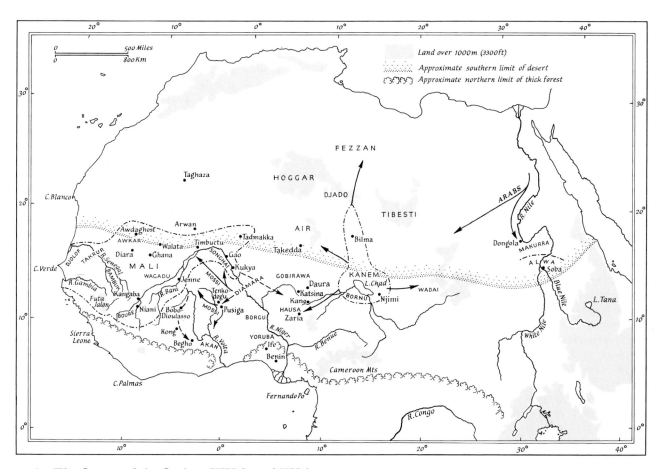

18 The States of the Sudan, XIVth and XVth Centuries

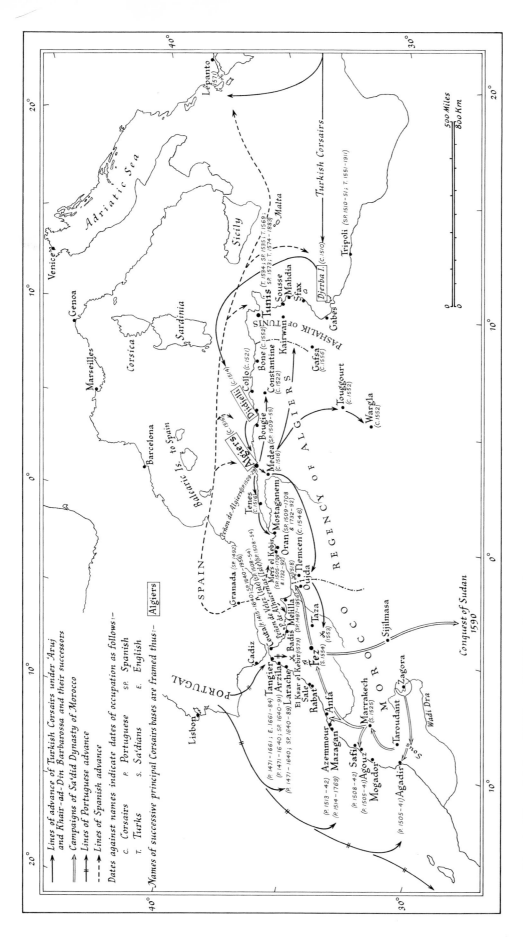

19 North-West Africa, XVth and XVIth Centuries

During the XVth century, with the expansion of Portugal, involving not only maritime expansion (Map 28) but also an attempt to conquer Morocco, initiative in the disunited Maghrib began to pass into the hands of outsiders. This process was intensified in the XVIth century when, after the Iberian Muslims had been finally expelled from the Iberian peninsula (1492), the Maghrib became involved in the struggle between Spain and the Ottoman Turks for control of the western Mediterranean. The maritime struggle ended in a formal victory for Spain at the Battle of Lepanto (1571), but in the course of it corsairs in the Ottoman service gained control of the African coastline from Egypt to the border of Morocco. Tripoli and Tunisia became Ottoman provinces. The central Maghrib (Algeria) was nom-inally under Ottoman suzerainty, but real power rested with the corsairs, who held the ports and sought to exploit the hinterland tribesmen. In the meantime the Portuguese attacks on Morocco had helped to stimulate the rise of its Saʻdid dynasty, which repulsed Portugal, kept out the Turks, and even aspired to the conquest of the western Sudan (see also Map 20).

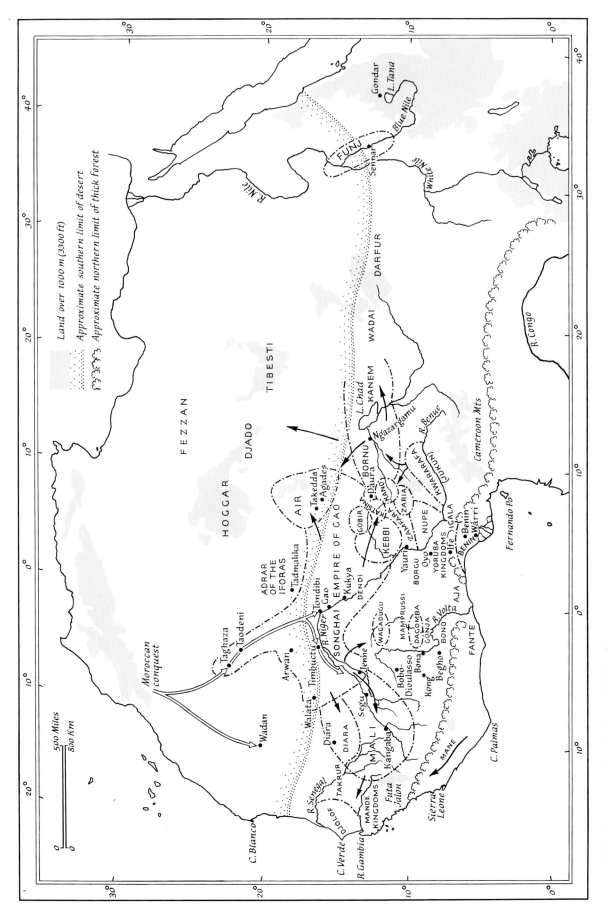

20   The States of the Sudan, XVIth Century

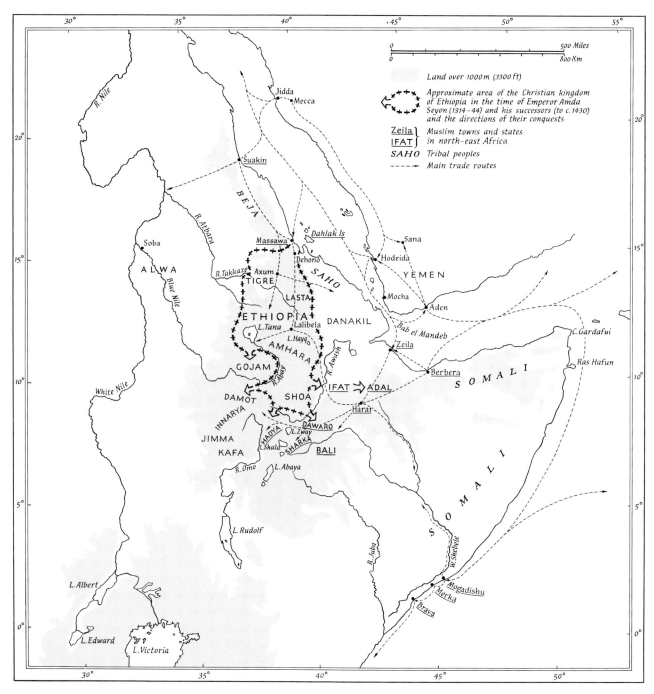

21 North-East Africa in the XIVth Century

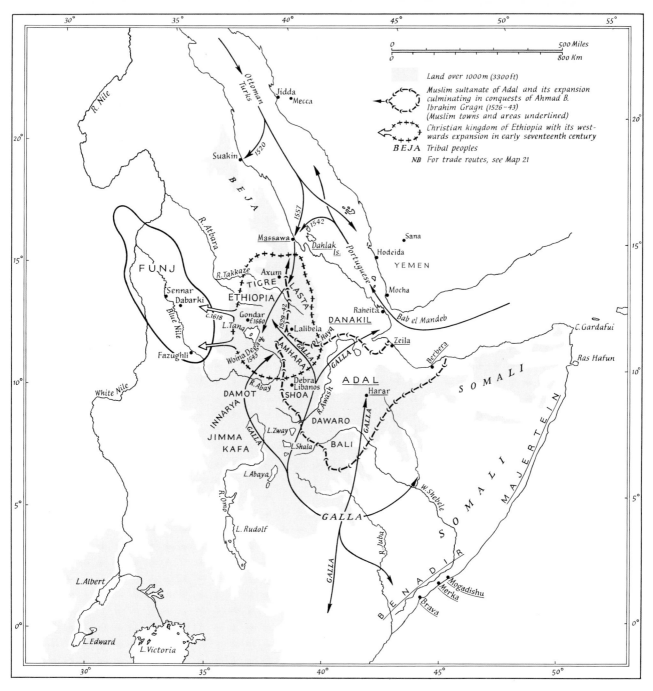

22 North-East Africa in the XVIth and XVIIth Centuries

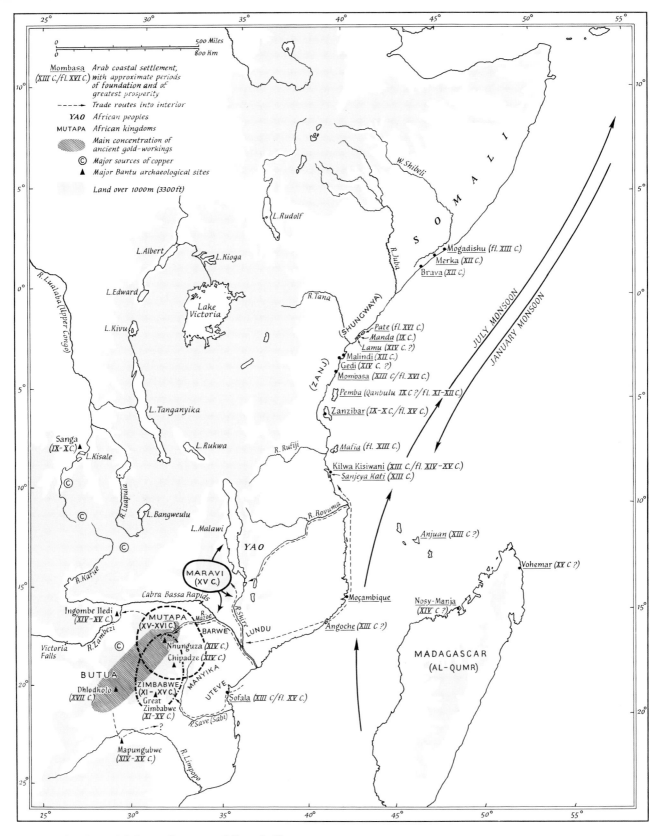

23 The East African Coast and South-East Africa, IXth Century to A.D. c.1500

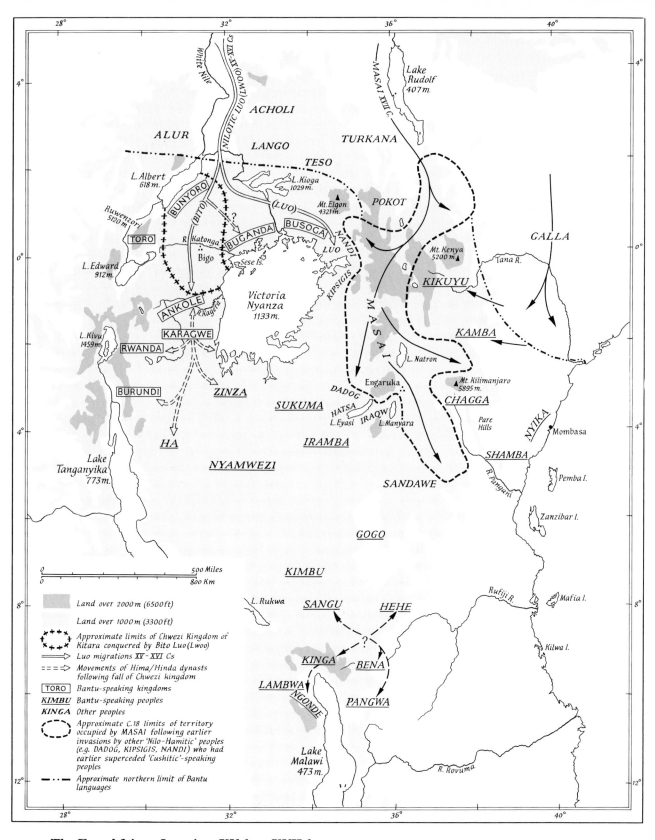

28° **32°** **36°** **40°**

White Nile

ACHOLI

ALUR
LANGO
TESO
TURKANA
Lake
Rudolf
407 m.

L. Albert
618 m.
L. Kioga
1029 m.
POKOT
GALLA

Ruwenzori
5120 m.
BUNYORO
(BITO)
Mt. Elgon
4321 m.
Mt. Kenya
5200 m.
Tana R.

TORO
R. Katonga
BUGANDA
BUSOGA
NANDI
KIKUYU

Bigo
LUO
L. Edward
912 m.
Sese Is.
KIPSIGIS
KAMBA

ANKOLE
R. Kagera
Victoria
Nyanza
1133 m.
MASAI

KARAGWE
L. Kivu
1459 m.
L. Natron
Mt. Kilimanjaro
5895 m.

RWANDA
ZINZA
DADOG
Engaruka
CHAGGA
Pare
Hills
NYIKA
Mombasa

BURUNDI
SUKUMA
HATSA
IRAQW
L. Eyasi
L. Manyara
SHAMBA
R. Pangani

HA
IRAMBA
Pemba I.

Lake
Tanganyika
773 m.
NYAMWEZI
SANDAWE
Zanzibar I.

GOGO

KIMBU
Rufiji R.
Mafia I.

0   500 Miles
0   800 Km
SANGU
HEHE

Land over 2000 m (6500 ft)
L. Rukwa
Kilwa I.

Land over 1000 m (3300 ft)
Approximate limits of Chwezi Kingdom of
Kitara conquered by Bito Luo (Lwoo)
KINGA
BENA

Luo migrations XV - XVI Cs
LAMBWA
NGONDE
PANGWA

Movements of Hima/Hinda dynasts
following fall of Chwezi kingdom

TORO Bantu-speaking kingdoms
KIMBU Bantu-speaking peoples
KINGA Other peoples
Approximate C.18 limits of territory
occupied by MASAI following earlier
invasions by other 'Nilo-Hamitic' peoples
(e.g. DADOG, KIPSIGIS, NANDI) who had
earlier superceded 'Cushitic'-speaking
peoples
Lake
Malawi
473 m.
R. Rovuma

Approximate northern limit of Bantu
languages

**24   The East African Interior, XVth to XVIIth
Centuries**

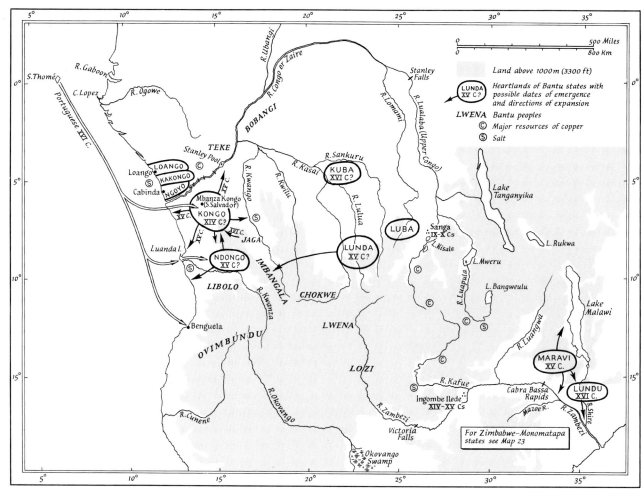

25 West Central Africa, XIVth to XVIth Centuries

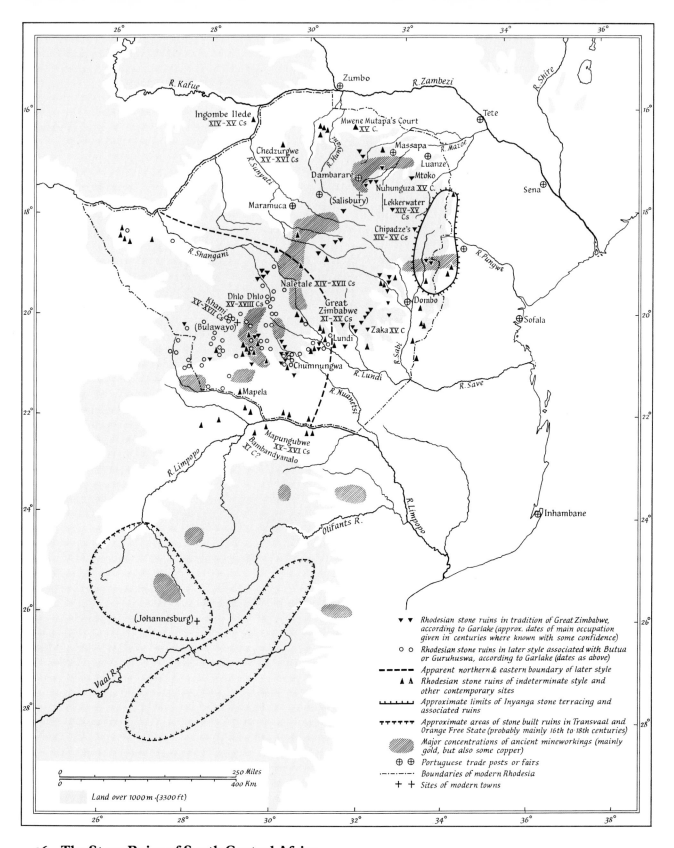

26 The Stone Ruins of South Central Africa

The distribution and typology of the Rhodesian ruins shown on this
map are based on figures 25 and 26 in Peter S. Garlake, *Great
Zimbabwe* (Thames and Hudson, 1973).

The following labels appear on the map:

R. Kafue
R. Zambezi
R. Shire
Zumbo
Ingombe Ilede XIV–XV Cs
Mwene Mutapa's Court XV C.
Tete
Chedzurgwe XV–XVI Cs
Massapa
R. Mazoe
Dambarare
Luanze
Mtoko
(Salisbury)
Nuhunguza XV C.
Sena
Maramuca
Lekkerwater XIV–XV Cs
Chipadze's XIV–XV Cs
R. Shangani
R. Pungwe
Naletale XIV–XVII Cs
Dombo
Dhlo Dhlo XV–XVIII Cs
Khami XV–XVII Cs
Great Zimbabwe XI–XV Cs
Sofala
(Bulawayo)
Lundi
Zaka XV C
Chumnungwa
R. Lundi
R. Save
Mapela
R. Nuanetsi
Mapungubwe XV–XVI Cs
Bambandyanalo XI C?
R. Limpopo
Inhambane
Olifants R.
R. Limpopo
(Johannesburg)
Vaal R.
Land over 1000 m (3300 ft)

0   250 Miles
0   400 Km

Legend:
▼ ▼ Rhodesian stone ruins in tradition of Great Zimbabwe,
according to Garlake (approx. dates of main occupation
given in centuries where known with some confidence)
○ ○ Rhodesian stone ruins in later style associated with Butua
or Guruhuswa, according to Garlake (dates as above)
– – – Apparent northern & eastern boundary of later style
▲ ▲ Rhodesian stone ruins of indeterminate style and
other contemporary sites
ⱅⱅⱅⱅ Approximate limits of Inyanga stone terracing and
associated ruins
ⱅⱅⱅⱅ Approximate areas of stone built ruins in Transvaal and
Orange Free State (probably mainly 16th to 18th centuries)
⬤ Major concentrations of ancient mineworkings (mainly
gold, but also some copper)
⊕ ⊕ Portuguese trade posts or fairs
–·–·– Boundaries of modern Rhodesia
+ + Sites of modern towns

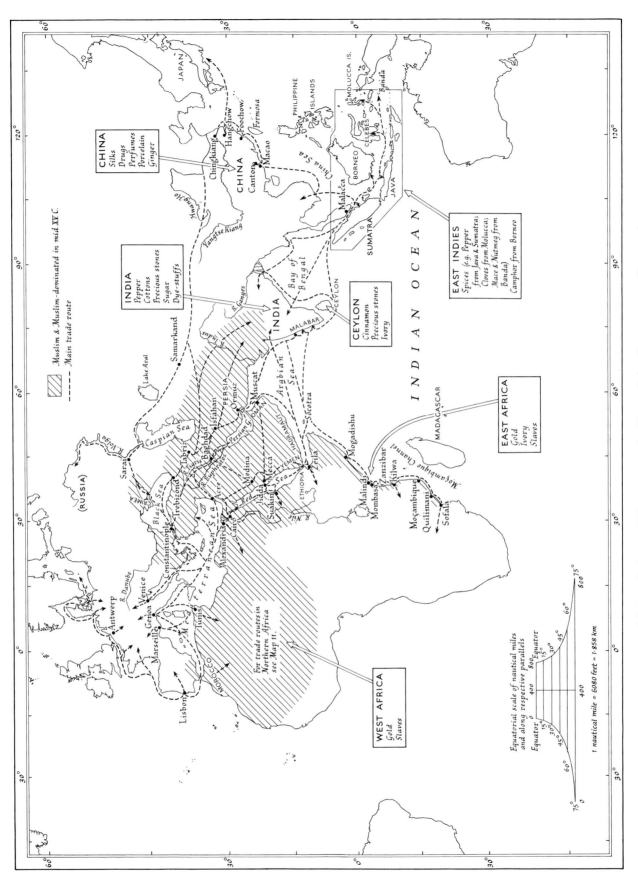

27 The Pattern of Trade between Africa, Asia and Europe on the Eve of the Portuguese Expansion

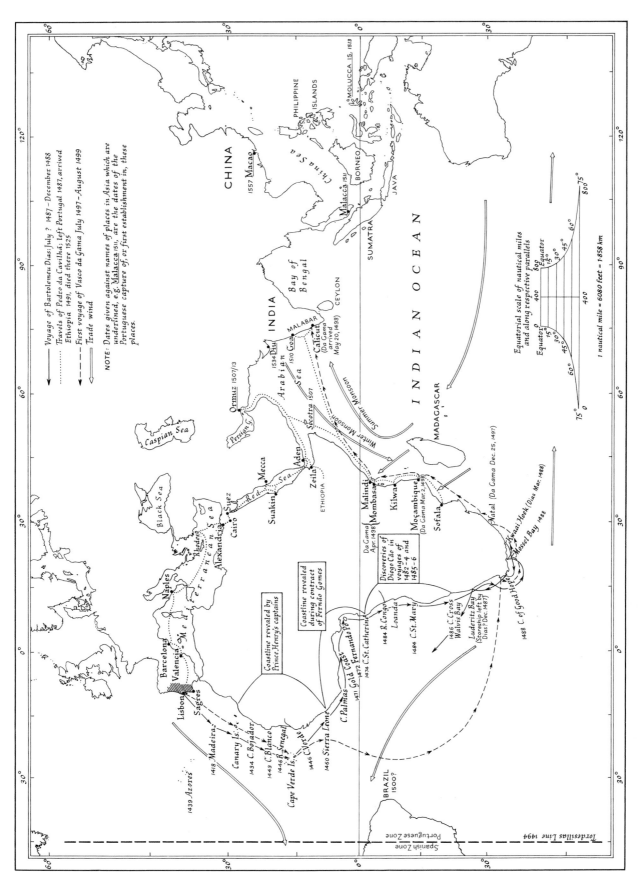

28 Portuguese Maritime Expansion, XVth to XVIth Centuries

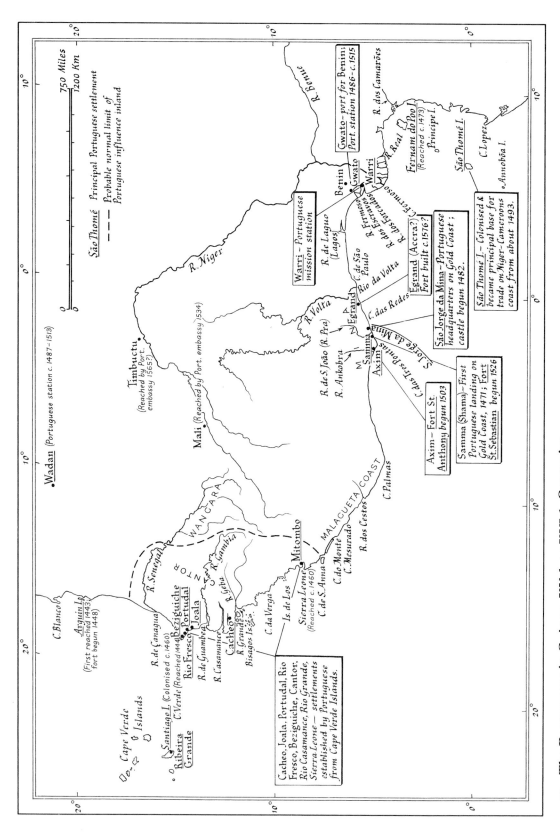

Cape Verde Islands

C. Blanco

Arguin I.
(First reached 1443;
fort begun 1448)

Santiago I. (Colonised c.1460)
Ribeira Grande

R. de Çanaguá
C. Verde (Reached 1444)
Beziguiche
Rio Fresco Portudal
R. de Guambea Joala
R. Casamance
Cacheo
R. Grande
Bisagos Is.

Wadan (Portuguese station c.1487–1513)

R. Senegal

WANGARA

C. da Verga

Is. de Los

Sierra Leone
(Reached c.1460)

C. de S. Anna

C. do Monte
C. Mesurado
R. dos Cestos
MALAGUETA COAST
C. Palmas

Mitombo

Timbuctu
(Reached by Port.
embassy 1565?)

R. Niger

Mali (Reached by Port. embassy 1534)

R. de S. João (R. Pra)
R. Ankobra
Axim
S. Jorge da Mina
Samma
C. das Puntas
M
Egrand
C. das Redes
R. Volta
Rio da Volta
C. de São Paulo
R. de Laguo
(Lagos)
Benin
Gwato
Warri

R. Benue

R. dos Camaroës

R. Real (Reached c.1473)
Principe I.

Fernam do Poo I.
(Reached c.1473)

São Thomé I.

C. Lopez

o Annobõa I.

Cacheo, Joala, Portudal, Rio
Fresco, Beziguiche, Cantor,
Rio Casamance, Rio Grande,
Sierra Leone — settlements
established by Portuguese
from Cape Verde Islands.

Axim – Fort St.
Anthony begun 1503

Samma (Shama) – First
Portuguese landing on
Gold Coast, 1471; Fort
St. Sebastian begun 1526

São Jorge da Mina – Portuguese
headquarters on Gold Coast;
castle begun 1482.

Egrand (Accra?)
Fort built c.1576?

São Thomé I. – Colonised &
became principal base for
trade on Niger-Cameroons
coast from about 1493.

Warri – Portuguese
mission station

Gwato – port for Benin:
Port. station 1486 – c.1515

R. dos Escravos
R. Fermoso
R. das Escravos

750 Miles
1200 Km

São Thomé   Principal Portuguese settlement
——— Probable normal limit of
     Portuguese influence inland

29   The Portuguese in Guinea, XVth to XVIth Centuries

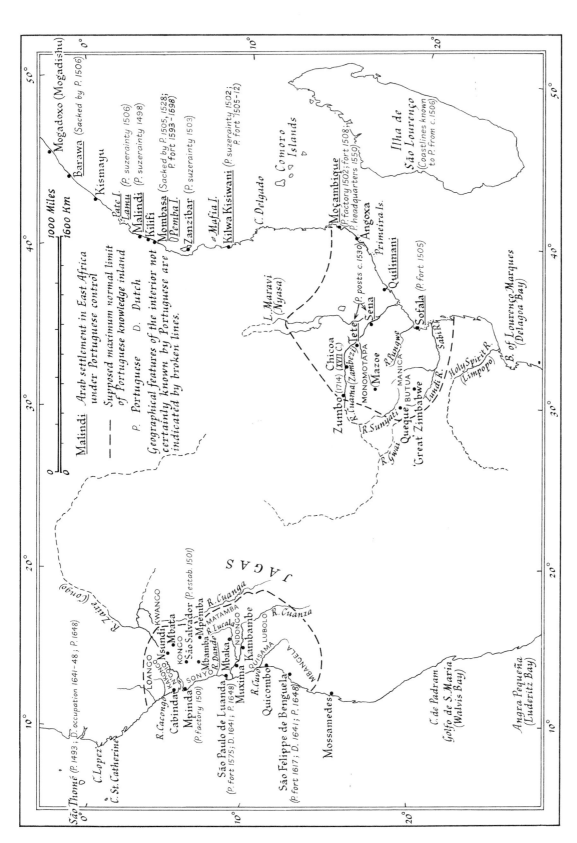

30 The Portuguese South of the Equator, XVth to XVIIth Centuries

Malindi   *Arab settlement in East Africa under Portuguese control*

– – –   *Supposed maximum normal limit of Portuguese knowledge inland*

P. *Portuguese*   D. *Dutch*

Geographical features of the interior not certainly known by Portuguese are indicated by broken lines.

1000 Miles
1600 Km

Mogadoxo (Mogadishu)
Barawa *(Sacked by P. 1506)*
Kismayu
Pate I. *(P. suzerainty 1506)*
Lamu
Malindi *(P. suzerainty 1498)*
Kilifi
Mombasa *(Sacked by P. 1505, 1528; P. fort 1593–1698)*
Pemba I.
Zanzibar *(P. suzerainty 1503)*
Mafia I.
Kilwa Kisiwani *(P. suzerainty 1502; P. fort 1505–12)*
C. Delgado
Comoro Islands
Moçambique *(P. factory 1502; fort 1508; P. headquarters 1550)*
Angoxa
Primeira Is.
Quilimani
Sofala *(P. fort 1505)*
Ilha de São Lourenço *(Coastlines known to P. from c. 1506)*
B. of Lourenço Marques *(Delagoa Bay)*

L. Maravi (Nyasa)
P. posts c. 1530
Sena
Tete
Chicoa *(XVII C.)*
Zumbo *(1714)*
R. Luama (Zambezi)
MONOMOTAPA
Mazoe
R. Luenya
MANICA
BUTUA
Great Zimbabwe
Queque
R. Sunjati
R. Gwai
Sabi R.
Lundi R.
Holy Spirit R. (Limpopo)

São Thomé *(P. 1493; D. occupation 1641–48; P. 1648)*
C. Lopez
C. St. Catherine
R. Zaïre (Congo)
LOANGO
KWANGO
R. Cacongo
Cabinda
NGOI
KAKONGO
Nsundi
Mbata
KONGO
São Salvador *(P. estab. 1501)*
Mpinda *(P. factory 1501)*
SONYO
R. Dande
Mbamba
Mpemba
Mbaka
MATAMBA
R. Lucala
NDONGO
Muxima
R. Cuanga
Kambambe
LUBOLO
R. Cuanza
QUISAMA
Quicombo
São Paulo de Luanda *(P. fort 1575; D. 1641; P. 1648)*
São Felippe de Benguela *(P. fort 1617; D. 1641; P. 1648)*
MBANELA
Mossamedes
C. de Padram
Golfo de S. Maria *(Walvis Bay)*
Angra Pequeña *(Lüderitz Bay)*

JAGAS

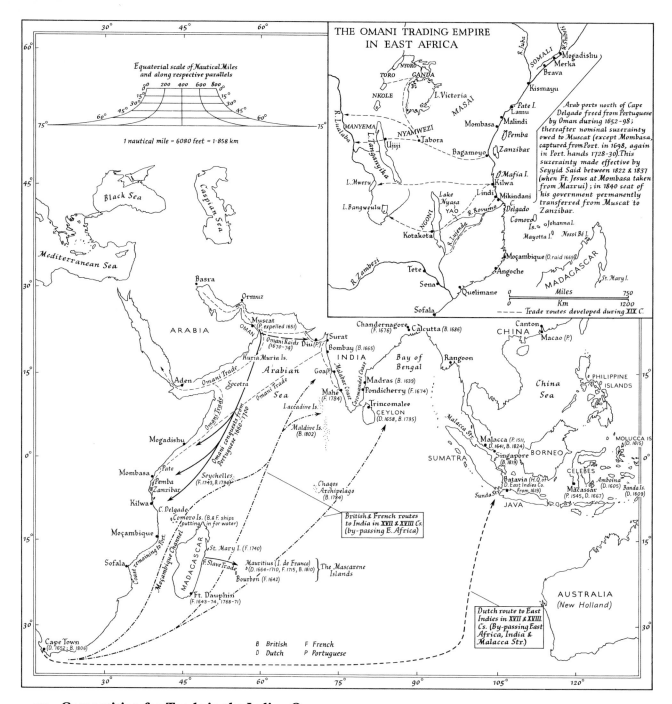

31 Competition for Trade in the Indian Ocean, XVIIth and XVIIIth Centuries

With the decline of the Portuguese power in the Indian Ocean, and the development of new sailing routes, first by the Dutch to the East Indies, and then by the English and French to India, the East African coast became neglected by European traders. North of Cape Delgado, the dominant commercial interest became that of Arabs from Oman (see Map 42). (For trade winds, see Map 28.)

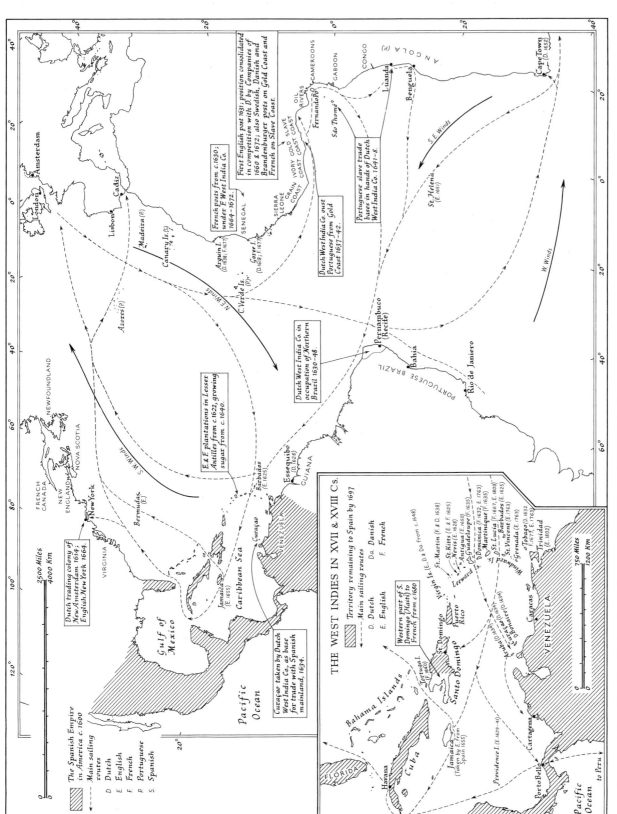

32 Competition for Trade in the Atlantic, XVIIth and XVIIIth Centuries

This map shows the relation between European activities in West Africa and in tropical America. Having conquered part of northern Brazil from the Portuguese, the Dutch West India Company also acquired most of their bases in West Africa to ensure a supply of Negro slaves for the Brazilian sugar plantations. The Portuguese soon expelled the Dutch from Brazil and from many of their West African bases, but Dutch destruction of Spanish naval power in American waters had enabled English and French colonists to settle in the Carribean. The Dutch encouraged the latter to embark on sugar planting and supplied the capital and slaves needed. In the latter part of the XVIIth century, as part of their reaction against Dutch domination of Atlantic trade, the English and French entered the slave-trade and acquired West African bases. Thereafter, Anglo-French rivalry in the West Indies is reflected in competition for the slave-trade and for the bases from which slaves were exported.

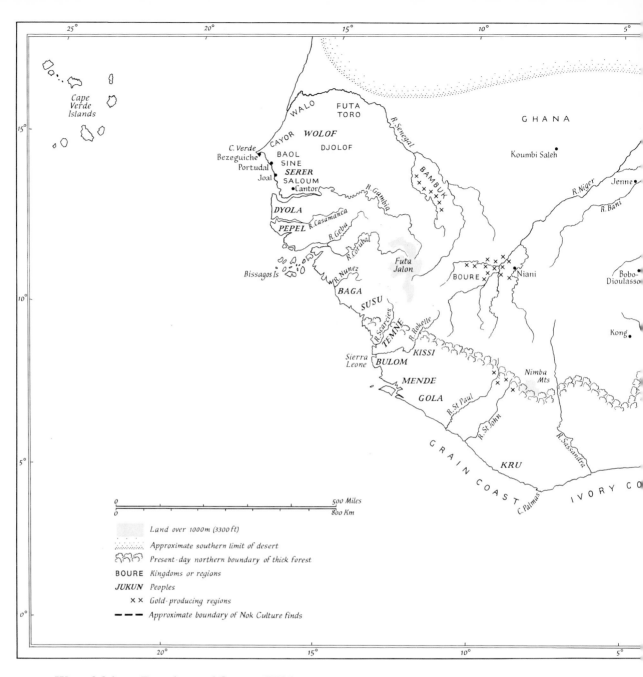

33   West African Peoples and States, XVth to XVIIth Centuries

Map labels:

Cape Verde Islands

GHANA

WALO
FUTA TORO
CAYOR
WOLOF
DJOLOF
R. Senegal
Koumbi Saleh
BAMBUK
R. Niger
Jenne
C. Verde
Bezeguiche
Portudal
Joal
BAOL
SINE
SERER
SALOUM
Cantor
R. Gambia
R. Bani
DYOLA
R. Casamanca
PEPEL
R. Gebu
R. Corubal
Futa Jalon
BOURE
Niani
Bobo-Dioulasso
Bissagos Is
R. Nunez
BAGA
SUSU
Kong
R. Scarcies
TEMNE
R. Rokelle
KISSI
Sierra Leone
BULOM
Nimba Mts
MENDE
GOLA
R. St Paul
R. St John
R. Sassandra
GRAIN COAST
KRU
C. Palmas
IVORY CO

Legend:

0 — 500 Miles
0 — 800 Km

Land over 1000m (3300 ft)

Approximate southern limit of desert

Present-day northern boundary of thick forest

BOURE Kingdoms or regions

JUKUN Peoples

× × Gold-producing regions

– – – Approximate boundary of Nok Culture finds

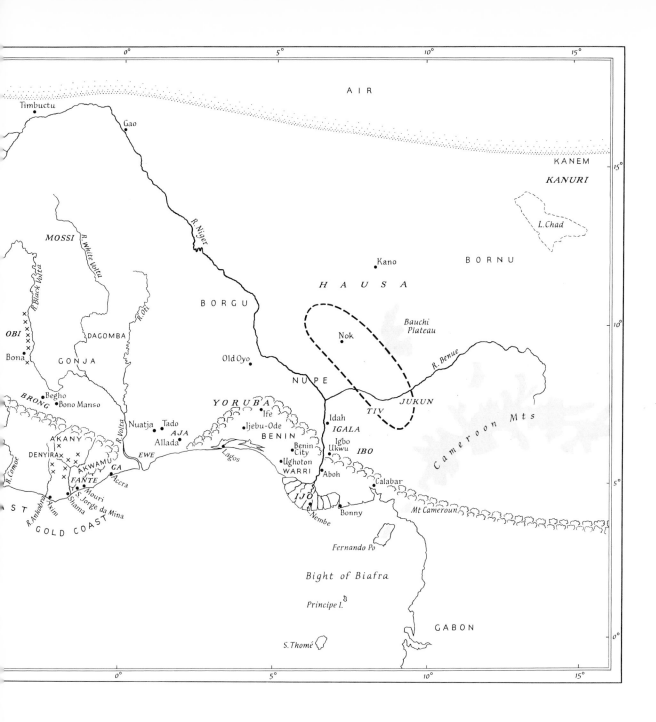

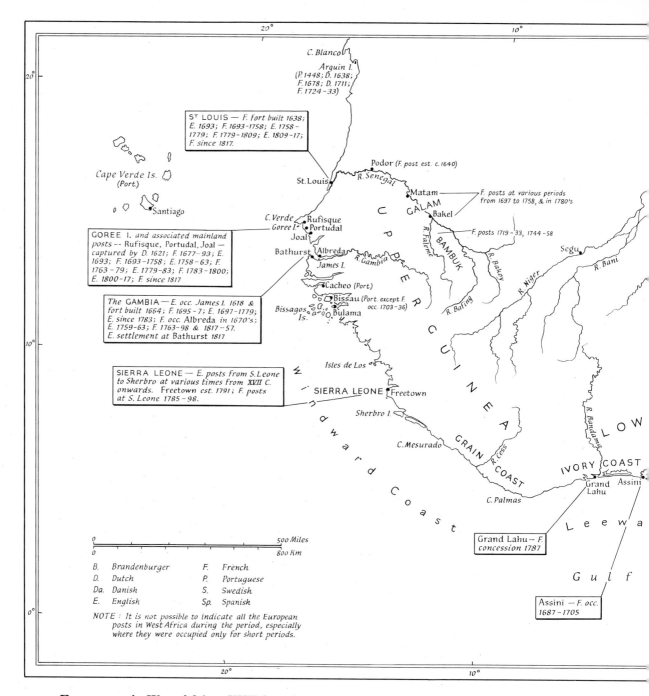

Arguin I.
(P. 1448; D. 1638;
F. 1678; D. 1711;
F. 1724-33)

ST LOUIS — F. fort built 1638;
E. 1693; F. 1693-1758; E. 1758-
1779; F. 1779-1809; E. 1809-17;
F. since 1817.

Podor (F. post est. c.1640)

F. posts at various periods
from 1697 to 1758, & in 1780's

Cape Verde Is. (Port.)

Santiago

C. Verde
Gorée I.
Joal

GOREE I. and associated mainland
posts -- Rufisque, Portudal, Joal --
captured by D. 1621; F. 1677-93; E.
1693; F. 1693-1758; E. 1758-63; F.
1763-79; E. 1779-83; F. 1783-1800;
E. 1800-17; F. since 1817

F. posts 1719-33, 1744-58

Segu

Bathurst
James I.

The GAMBIA — E. occ. James I. 1618 &
fort built 1664; F. 1695-7; E. 1697-1779;
E. since 1783; F. occ. Albreda in 1670's;
E. 1759-63; F. 1763-98 & 1817-57.
E. settlement at Bathurst 1817

Cacheo (Port.)

Bissau (Port. except F.
occ. 1703-36)

Bissagos
Is.

Bulama

SIERRA LEONE — E. posts from S. Leone
to Sherbro at various times from XVII C.
onwards. Freetown est. 1791; F. posts
at S. Leone 1785-98.

Isles de Los

SIERRA LEONE Freetown

Sherbro I.

C. Mesurado

C. Palmas

IVORY COAST
Grand   Assini
Lahu

Grand Lahu — F.
concession 1787

Assini — F. occ.
1687-1705

500 Miles

800 Km

B.	Brandenburger	F.	French
D.	Dutch	P.	Portuguese
Da.	Danish	S.	Swedish
E.	English	Sp.	Spanish

NOTE: It is not possible to indicate all the European
posts in West Africa during the period, especially
where they were occupied only for short periods.

34   Europeans in West Africa, XVIIth and XVIIIth Centuries

Note that, with the exception of the French attempts to develop trade up the River Senegal, attracted in part by its gold resources, European interests in West Africa during this period were confined to coastal trading bases from which slaves could be bought for export to America. While the French concentrated on the Senegal and Upper Guinea, English and Dutch companies competed for the better-established trade of the Gold Coast, with the result that this was the scene of the greatest concentration of European forts in West Africa. As the demand for slaves increased, it was met principally by extending the field of trading operations farther east into the Gulf of Guinea and beyond. Here trade was conducted on the European side by individuals rather than by chartered companies, and permanent forts of the Gold Coast type were not built.

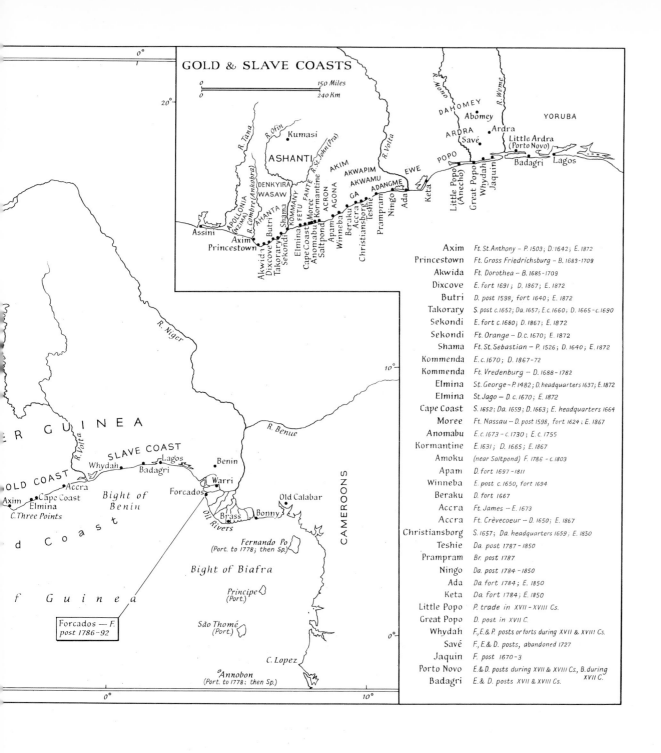

GOLD & SLAVE COASTS

Axim	Ft. St. Anthony – P. 1503; D. 1642; E. 1872
Princestown	Ft. Gross Friedrichsburg – B. 1683-1709
Akwida	Ft. Dorothea – B. 1685-1709
Dixcove	E. fort 1691; D. 1867; E. 1872
Butri	D. post 1598, fort 1640; E. 1872
Takorary	S. post c.1652; Da. 1657; E.c. 1660; D. 1665 - c. 1690
Sekondi	E. fort c. 1680; D. 1867; E. 1872
Sekondi	Ft. Orange – D.c. 1670; E. 1872
Shama	Ft. St. Sebastian – P. 1526; D. 1640; E. 1872
Kommenda	E. c. 1670; D. 1867-72
Kommenda	Ft. Vredenburg – D. 1688-1782
Elmina	St. George – P. 1482; D. headquarters 1637; E. 1872
Elmina	St. Jago – D. c. 1670; E. 1872
Cape Coast	S. 1652; Da. 1659; D. 1663; E. headquarters 1664
Moree	Ft. Nassau – D. post 1598, fort 1624; E. 1867
Anomabu	E. c. 1673 - c. 1730; E. c. 1755
Kormantine	E. 1631; D. 1665; E. 1867
Amoku	(near Saltpond) F. 1786 - c. 1803
Apam	D. fort 1697-1811
Winneba	E. post c. 1650, fort 1694
Beraku	D. fort 1667
Accra	Ft. James – E. 1673
Accra	Ft. Crèvecoeur – D. 1650; E. 1867
Christiansborg	S. 1657; Da. headquarters 1659; E. 1850
Teshie	Da. post 1787 - 1850
Prampram	Br. post 1787
Ningo	Da. post 1784 - 1850
Ada	Da. fort 1784; E. 1850
Keta	Da. fort 1784; E. 1850
Little Popo	P. trade in XVII - XVIII Cs.
Great Popo	D. post in XVII C.
Whydah	F., E. & P. posts or forts during XVII & XVIII Cs.
Savé	F., E. & D. posts, abandoned 1727
Jaquin	F. post 1670-3
Porto Novo	E. & D. posts during XVII & XVIII Cs., B. during XVII C.
Badagri	E. & D. posts XVII & XVIII Cs.

Forcados — F. post 1786-92

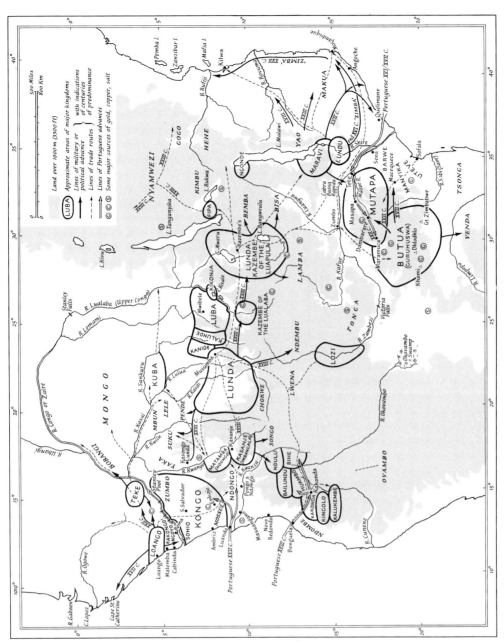

35 Bantu Africa from the Congo to the Limpopo, XVIIth and XVIIIth Centuries

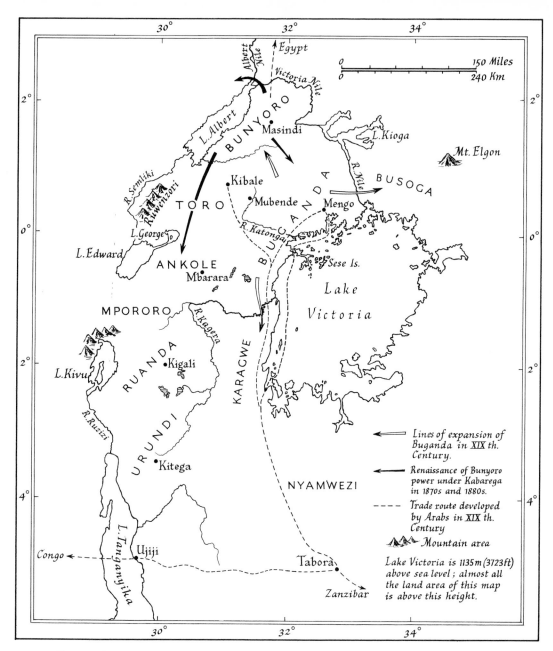

36 Bantu States of the Great Lakes, XVIIIth and XIXth Centuries

This map should be viewed in conjunction with Map 24 on which is shown the Kitara empire established by the Chwezi, one of the Hima clans, during the XIIIth, XIVth, and XVth centuries. During the late XVth century the Chwezi were ousted by the Bito clan of the Luo (or Lwoo), who set up the still-surviving kingdoms of Bunyoro, Buganda, and Busoga. Farther south however, Hima or Hinda dynasties managed to hold out, in Ankole, Ruanda, Urundi, and Karagwe, and eventually to stem the Luo advance. In the north Bunyoro became the effective successor to Kitara, though from the second half of the XVIIIth century onwards the power and extent of its kingdom declined, and Buganda, which was better situated to benefit from the mid-XIXth century extension of Arab trade from the east coast, became the more powerful kingdom.

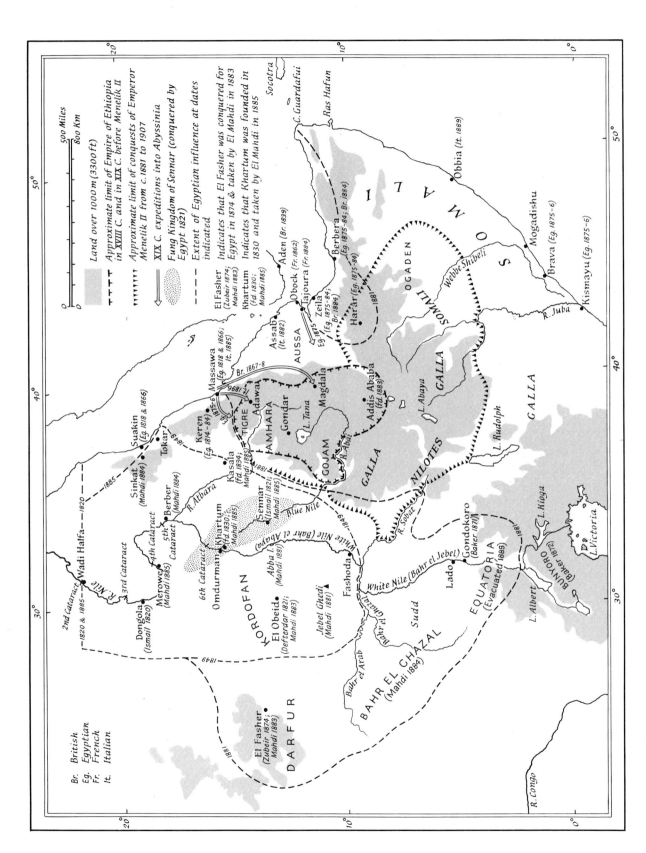

Land over 1000 m (3300 ft)

Approximate limit of Empire of Ethiopia in XVIII C. and in XIX C. before Menelik II

Approximate limit of conquests of Emperor Menelik II from c.1881 to 1907

XIX C. expeditions into Abyssinia

Fung Kingdom of Sennar (conquered by Egypt 1821)

Extent of Egyptian influence at dates indicated

El Fasher (Zubeir 1874; Mahdi 1883) — Indicates that El Fasher was conquered for Egypt in 1874 & taken by El Mahdi in 1883

Khartum (fd. 1830; Mahdi 1885) — Indicates that Khartum was founded in 1830 and taken by El Mahdi in 1885

Br. British
Eg. Egyptian
Fr. French
It. Italian

SOMALI
OGADEN
ITALI
GALLA
AMHARA
TIGRE
GOJAM
NILOTES
KORDOFAN
DARFUR
BAHR EL GHAZAL
EQUATORIA (Evacuated 1889)
BUNYORO

Socotra

C. Guardafui

Ras Hafun

Obbia (It. 1889)

Mogadishu

Brava (Eg. 1875–6)

Kismayu (Eg. 1875–6)

R. Juba

Webbe Shibeli

Aden (Br. 1839)

Berbera (Eg. 1875–84; Br. 1884)

Harar 1881

Zeila (Eg. 1875–84; Br. 1884)

Tajoura (Fr. 1884)

Obock (Fr. 1862)

Assab (It. 1882)

AUSSA

Massawa (Eg. 1818 & 1866; It. 1885)

Keren (Eg. 1814–84)

Br. 1867–8

1868?

1875–6

Adawa

Gondar

Magdala (fd. 1883)

L. Tana

Addis Ababa (fd. 1883)

L. Abaya

R. Abai

L. Rudolph

L. Kioga

L. Victoria

L. Albert

Gondokoro (Baker 1871)

Lado

White Nile (Bahr el Jebel)

1849

R. Sobat

Bahr el Ghazal

Bahr el Arab

Sudd

Fashoda

White Nile (Bahr el Abaya)

Blue Nile

Sennar (Ismail 1821; Mahdi 1885)

Abba I. (Mahdi 1881)

Jebel Ghedi (Mahdi 1881)

El Obeid (Defterdar 1821; Mahdi 1883)

Omdurman

Khartum (fd. 1830; Mahdi 1885)

6th Cataract

Merowe (Mahdi 1885)

Dongola (Ismail 1820)

5th Cataract

4th Cataract

3rd Cataract

2nd Cataract

R. Nile

Wadi Halfa 1820

1820 & 1885

1885

Berber (Mahdi 1884)

Kasala (fd. 1834; Mahdi 1885)

R. Atbara

Tokar

Sinkat (Mahdi 1884)

Suakin (Eg. 1818 & 1866)

R. Congo

El Fasher (Zubeir 1874; Mahdi 1883)

1881

500 Miles
800 Km

20°
10°
0°
50°
40°
30°
20°
10°
0°

BUNYORO (Baker 1872)

37   North-East Africa, XVIIth to XIXth Centuries

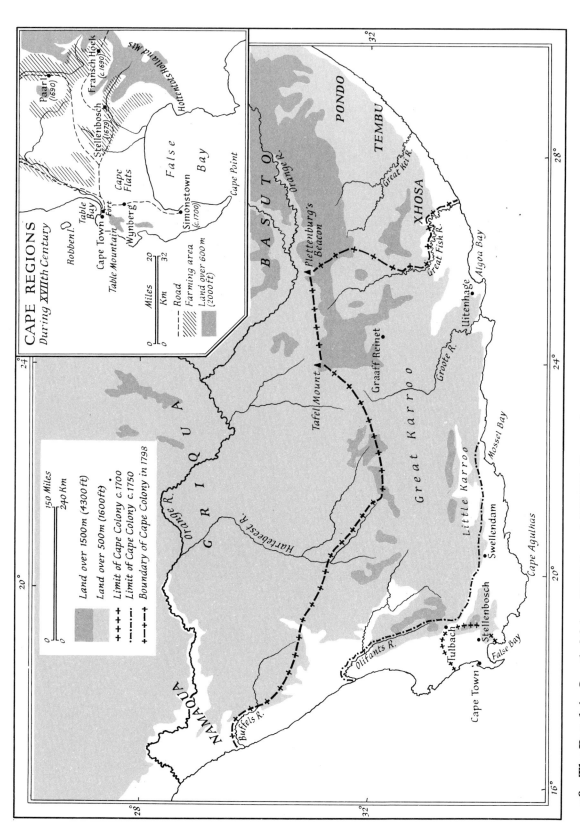

CAPE REGIONS
During XVIIIth Century

Miles
Km

Road
Farming area
Land over 600 m
(2000 ft)

Robben I.
Table
Bay
Cape Town
Fort
Wynberg
Simonstown
(c.1700)
Cape Point
Table Mountain
Cape
Flats
F a l s e
B a y
Paarl
(1690)
Stellenbosch
(1679)
Fransch Hoek
(c.1690)
Hottentots Holland Mts
Hottentots Holland Mts

150 Miles
240 Km

Land over 1500 m (4300 ft)
Land over 500 m (1600 ft)
Limit of Cape Colony c.1700
Limit of Cape Colony c.1750
Boundary of Cape Colony in 1798

N A M A Q U A
G R I Q U A
B A S U T O
PONDO
TEMBU
XHOSA

Orange R.
Buffels R.
Hartbeest R.
Orange R.
Olifants R.
Grovte R.
Great Fish R.
Great Kei R.

Tafel Mount.
Plettenburg's
Beacon
Graaff Reinet
Uitenhage
Algoa Bay
Mossel Bay
Little Karroo
G r e a t   K a r r o o
Swellendam
Cape Agulhas
Stellenbosch
Tulbach
Cape Town
False Bay

16°   20°   24°   28°   32°

28°   32°   24°   20°

38   The Dutch in South Africa, XVIIth and XVIIIth Centuries

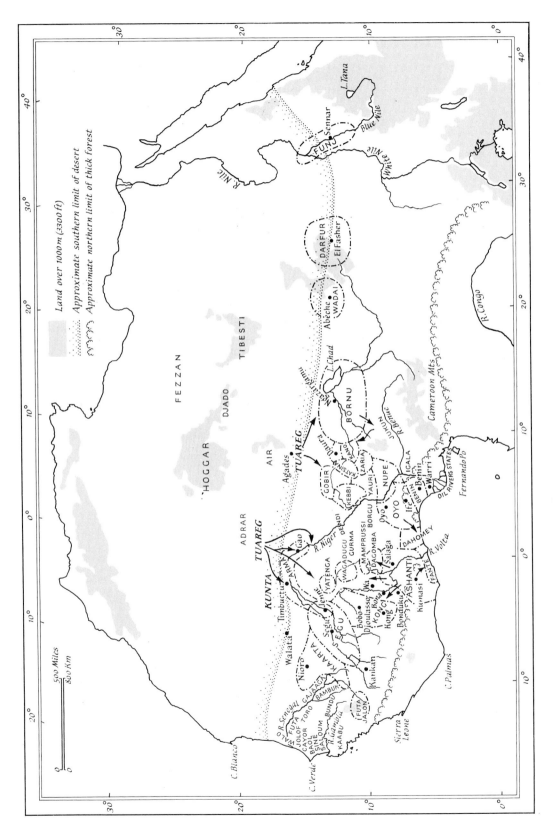

39   States of the Sudan and Guinea, XVIIIth Century

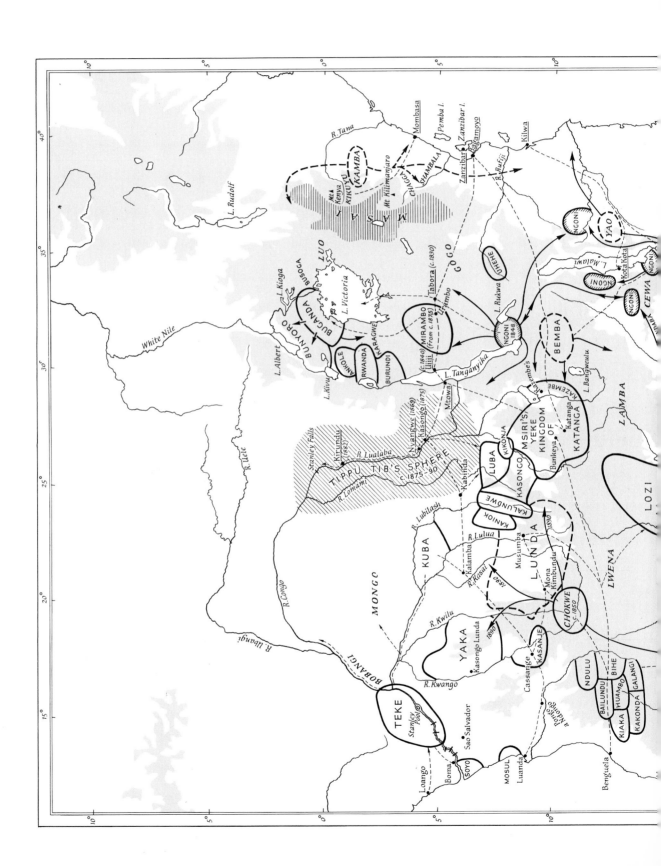

L. Rudolf

R. Tana

Mombasa

Pemba I.

Zanzibar I.

Bagamoyo

Kilwa

Mt. Kilimanjaro

Mt. Kenya

KIKUYU

(KAMBA)

SHAMBALA

CHAGGA

M A S A I

L. Kioga

L. Victoria

LUO

BUSOGA

BUGANDA

BUNYORO

L. Albert

White Nile

R. Uéle

L. Kivu

NKOLE

KARAGWE

RWANDA

BURUNDI

Tabora (c. 1830)

Tambo

GOGO

MIRAMBO
(from c. 1875)
(c. 1840)
Ujiji

UHEHE

L. Rukwa

NGONI

L. Tanganyika

Rungu's

Itembe's

L. Malawi

YAO

NGONI

Kota Kota

NGONI

NGONI

CEWA

MPATA

BEMBA

L. Bangweulu

Stanley Falls

Kirundu
(1887)

Nyangwe (1869)

Kasongo (1875)

Mtowa

R. Lualaba

R. Lomami

TIPPU TIB'S SPHERE
c. 1875-90

LAMBA

KAZEMBE

Katanga

MSIRI'S

YEKE

KINGDOM

OF

KATANGA

LUBA

KIKONJA

KASONGO

Kabinda

KUBA

MONGO

R. Congo

R. Lubilash

R. Lulua

R. Kasai

Musumba

Mona
Kimbundu

1890

KANIOK

KALUNDWE

LUNDA

LWENA

LOZI

CHOKWE
c. 1850

1890

R. Ubangi

BOBANGI

R. Kwilu

YAKA

Kasongo Lunda

R. Kwango

R. Kalamba

Cassange

KASANJE

Pungo a
Ndongo

NDULU

BAILUNDU

HUAMBO

BIHE

GALANGI

KIAKA

KAKONDA

TEKE

Stanley
Pool

Sao Salvador

MOSUL

Loango

Boma

SOYO

Luanda

Benguela

R. Rufiji

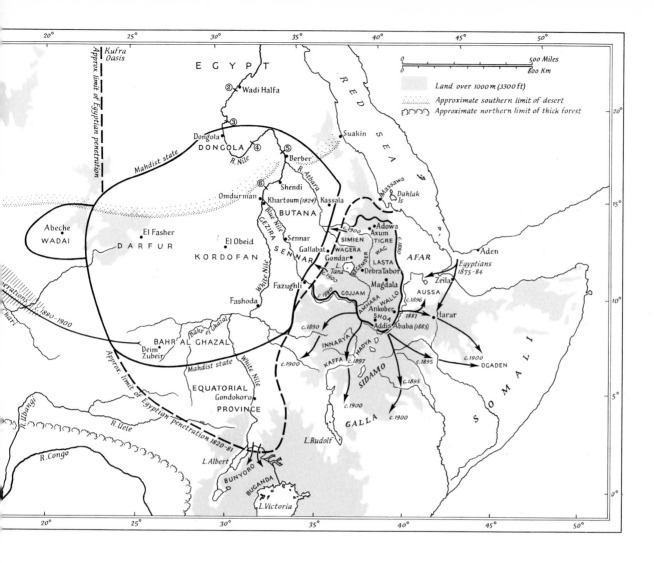

Map legend

Land over 1000m (3300 ft)

Approximate southern limit of desert

Approximate northern limit of thick forest

500 Miles
800 Km

Place names and labels

Kufra Oasis

Approx limit of Egyptian penetration

EGYPT

② Wadi Halfa

③

Dongola

DONGOLA ④ ⑤ Berber

R. Nile

Mahdist state

⑥ Shendi

Omdurman • Khartoum (1824)

Suakin

RED SEA

Massawa • Dahlak Is

Abeche WADAI

El Fasher

DARFUR

KORDOFAN

El Obeid

Sennar

Gallabat

SENNAR

GEZIRA

Blue Nile

BUTANA

Kassala

c.1900

SIMIEN
WAGERA
Gondar
L. Tana
BEGEMDER
DebraTabor

Adowa • Axum
TIGRE
WAG
LASTA
AFAR
c.1880

Aden

Egyptians 1875-84

Zeila

White Nile

Fazughli

c.1880

GOJJAM

Magdala

AUSSA

c.1896

Fashoda

c.1890

BAHR AL GHAZAL

Bahr el Ghazal

AMHARA
Ankober
SHOA
Addis Ababa (1883)
WALLO
1887

Harar

operations c.1880-1900

Chari

Deim Zubeir

Mahdist state

White Nile

Approx limit of Egyptian penetration 1820-81

EQUATORIAL PROVINCE

Gondokoro

c.1890
INNARYA
KAFFA c.1897
HADYA
SIDAMO
c.1895

c.1895

c.1900 OGADEN

SOMALI

R. Ubangi

R. Uele

L. Rudolf

GALLA c.1900

c.1900

R. Congo

L. Albert

BUNYORO
BUGANDA
L. Victoria

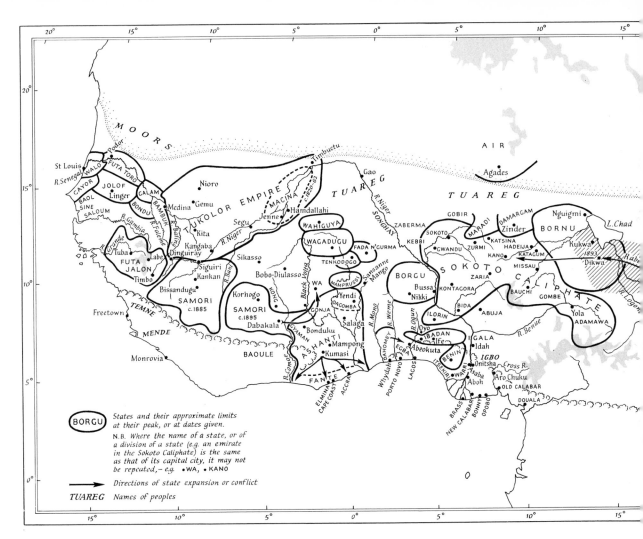

41 States of the Sudan, Ethiopia and Guinea in the XIXth Century

Legend (on map):

(BORGU) States and their approximate limits at their peak, or at dates given.

N.B. Where the name of a state, or of a division of a state (e.g. an emirate in the Sokoto Caliphate) is the same as that of its capital city, it may not be repeated,– e.g. •WA, •KANO

→ Directions of state expansion or conflict

TUAREG Names of peoples

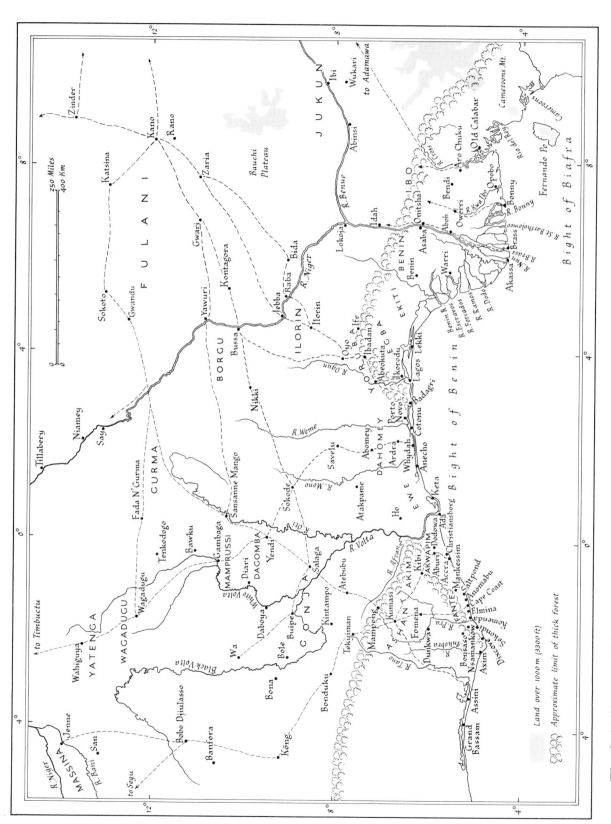

40   The Gold Coast and Nigeria in the XIXth Century

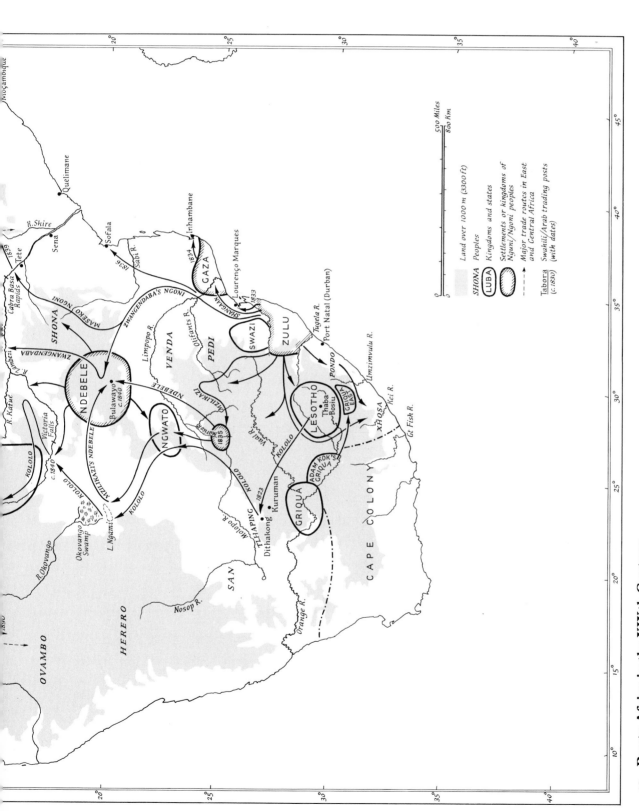

Land over 1000 m (3300 ft)

SHONA   Peoples

⬭LUBA⬭   Kingdoms and states

Settlements or kingdoms of
Nguni/Ngoni peoples

Major trade routes in East
and Central Africa

Tabora   Swahili/Arab trading posts
(c.1830)   (with dates)

0   500 Miles
0   800 Km

42   Bantu Africa in the XIXth Century

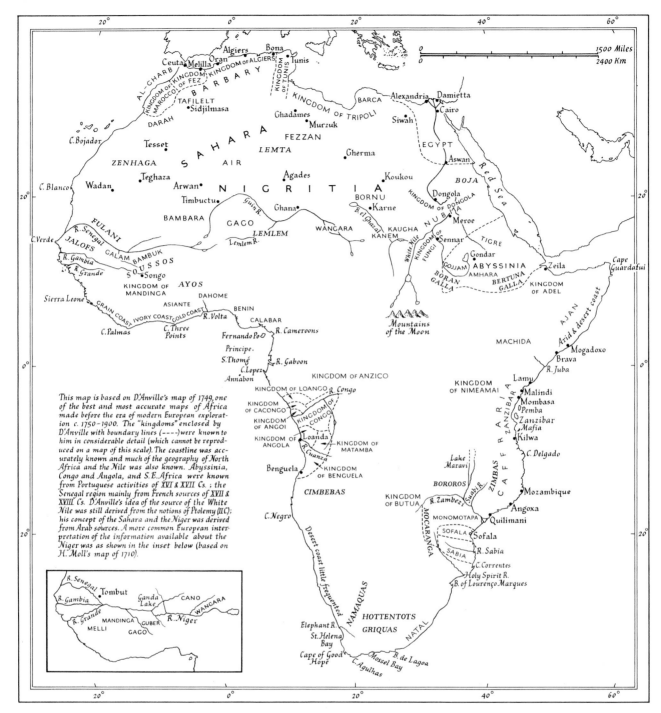

This map is based on D'Anville's map of 1749, one of the best and most accurate maps of Africa made before the era of modern European exploration c. 1750–1900. The "kingdoms" enclosed by D'Anville with boundary lines (––––) were known to him in considerable detail (which cannot be reproduced on a map of this scale). The coastline was accurately known and much of the geography of North Africa and the Nile was also known. Abyssinia, Congo and Angola, and S.E. Africa were known from Portuguese activities of XVI & XVII Cs.; the Senegal region mainly from French sources of XVII & XVIII Cs. D'Anville's idea of the source of the White Nile was still derived from the notions of Ptolemy (IIC); his concept of the Sahara and the Niger was derived from Arab sources. A more common European interpretation of the information available about the Niger was as shown in the inset below (based on H. Moll's map of 1710).

43 Africa as Known to Europeans in the Mid-XVIIIth Century

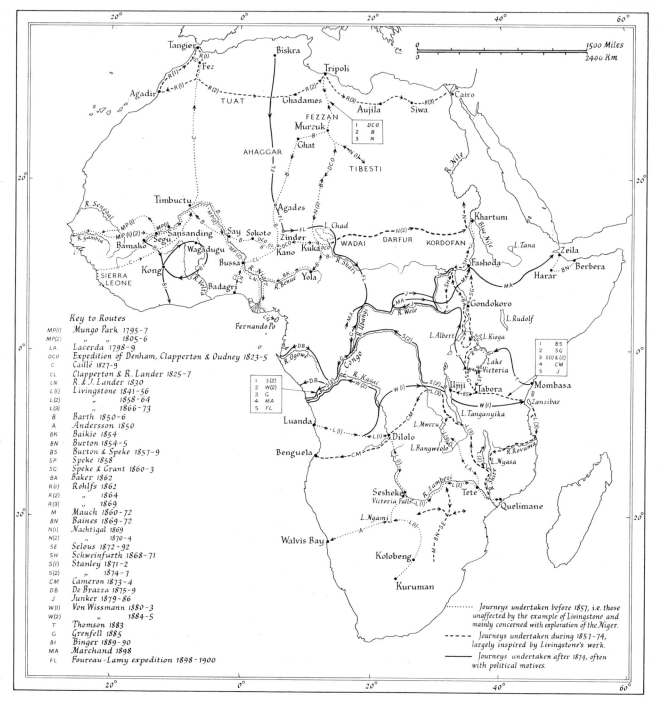

44   The European Exploration of Africa, 1788–1900

It is impossible on a map of this scale to show all the journeys which made appreciable new contributions to Europe's geographical knowledge of the African continent. An attempt has been made, however, to show those journeys of major historical importance. The extent to which these were concerned, until 1874 at least, with the elucidation of the major internal waterways is noteworthy.

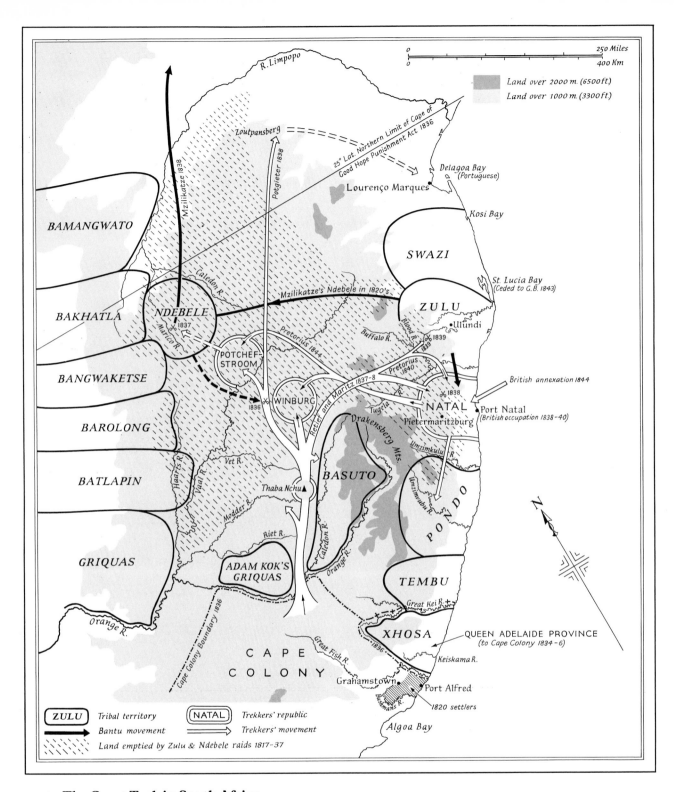

45   The Great Trek in South Africa

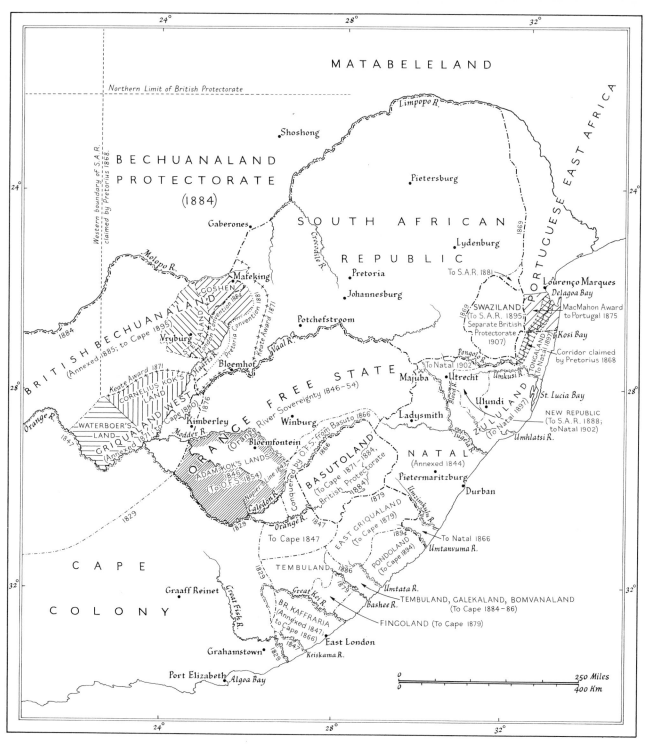

46 Frontier Changes in South-East Africa in the XIXth Century

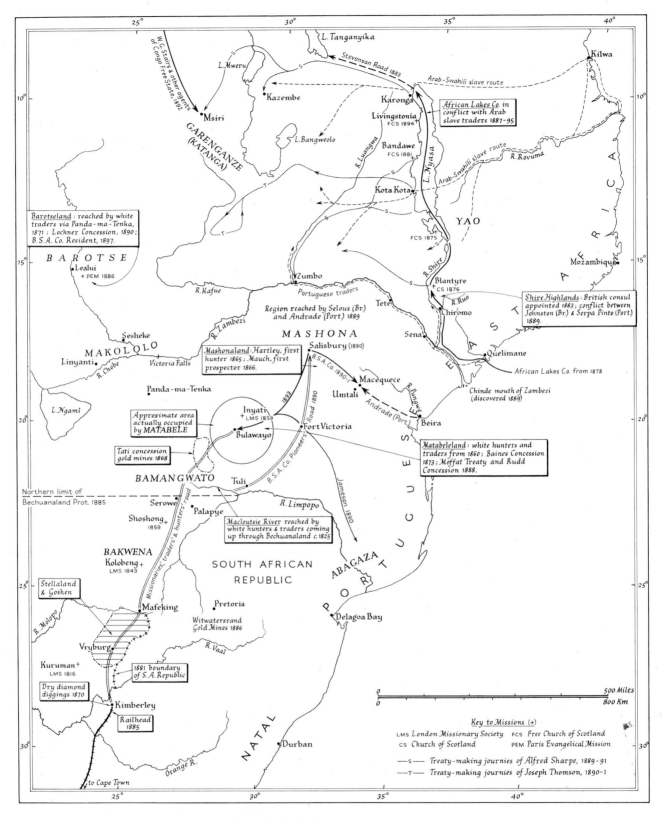

47 **Expansion of European Trade and Christian
Missions in Central and East Africa, 1843–97**
(see opposite)

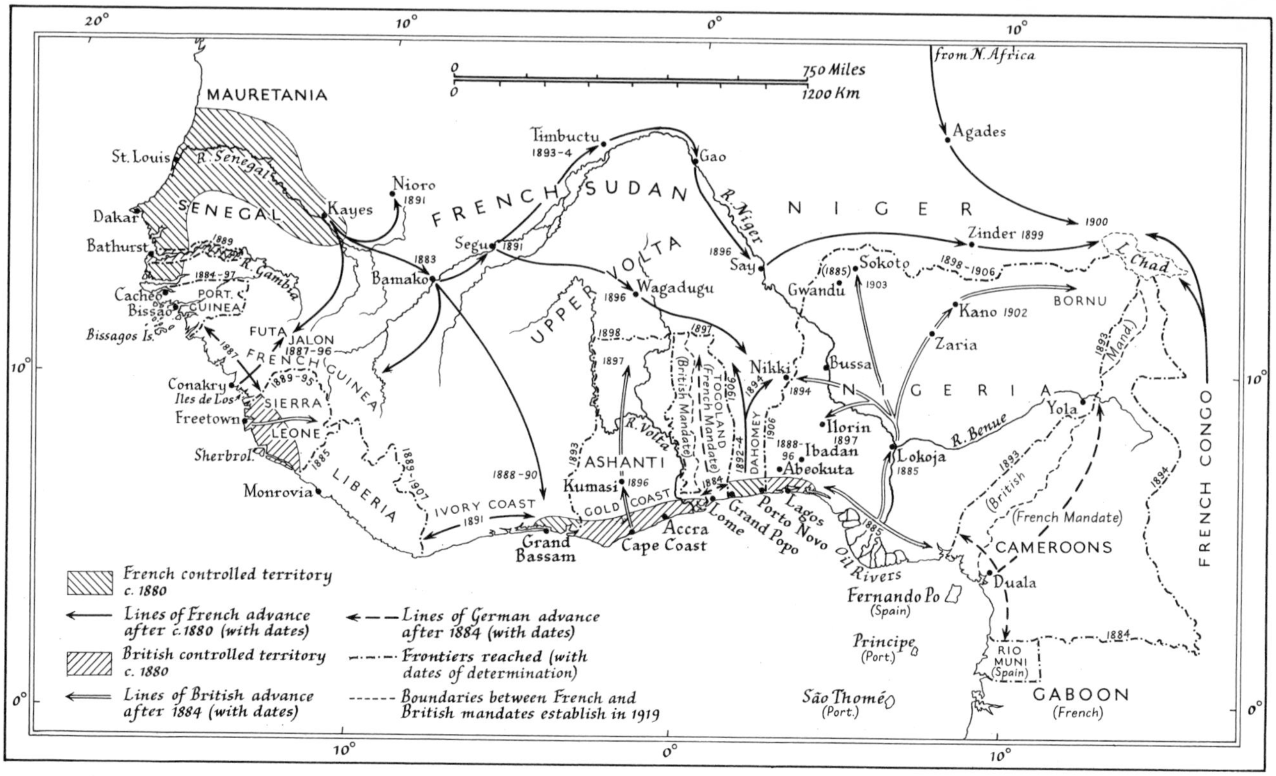

MAURETANIA
St. Louis
R. Senegal
Dakar
SENEGAL
Kayes
Bathurst
R. Gambia
Cacheo
Bissao
PORT. GUINEA
Bissagos Is.
FUTA JALON 1887-96
FRENCH GUINEA
Conakry
Iles de Los
SIERRA LEONE
Freetown
Sherbro I.
Monrovia
LIBERIA
Nioro 1891
FRENCH SUDAN
Segu 1891
Bamako 1883
Timbuctu 1893-4
Gao
R. Niger
NIGER
Say 1896
Wagadugu 1896
UPPER VOLTA
R. Volta
ASHANTI
Kumasi 1896
GOLD COAST
IVORY COAST 1891
Grand Bassam
Cape Coast
Accra
TOGOLAND (British Mandate) (French Mandate)
DAHOMEY
Lome
Grand Popo
Porto Novo
Lagos
Abeokuta
Ibadan
Ilorin
Nikki 1894
Bussa
Gwandu
Sokoto
Kano 1902
Zaria
NIGERIA
Lokoja 1885
R. Benue
Oil Rivers
Yola
BORNU
Zinder 1899
L. Chad
Agades
from N. Africa
CAMEROONS
(British) (French Mandate)
Duala
Fernando Po (Spain)
Principe (Port.)
São Thomé (Port.)
RIO MUNI (Spain)
GABOON (French)
FRENCH CONGO
750 Miles
1200 Km
French controlled territory c. 1880
Lines of French advance after c.1880 (with dates)
British controlled territory c. 1880
Lines of British advance after 1884 (with dates)
Lines of German advance after 1884 (with dates)
Frontiers reached (with dates of determination)
Boundaries between French and British mandates establish in 1919

48 The European Advance into West Africa

47 Expansion of European Trade and Christian Missions in Central and East Africa, 1843–97

Two main lines of penetration are shown. The first was northwards from the Cape Colony and began as a natural extension of the area of activity of its European settlers, with the journeys first of hunters, then of missionaries and traders. The emergence of the Boer republics with independent policies tended from the 1840s onwards to confine this line of advance to the narrow habitable strip of Botswana between the republics and the Kalahari desert. Up this channel towards the Zambezi pushed the missionaries, with Livingstone in the van, and a motley crowd of hunters, explorers, traders, and concession-seekers. By the 1880s, the whole of the area south of the Zambezi and north and west of the Boer republics had been opened up by such men, and missionaries and traders had also begun to penetrate Barotseland, but their activities still remained subject to the control of the native sovereigns. With the advent of Cecil Rhodes, all these various activities began to be combined under forceful political and economic leadership. The British political power engulfed Botswana (1884–5), and then in 1890 Rhodes's British South Africa Company extended the area of European settlement to the Zambezi and began to extend political power across the river into Barotseland. But the line of advance through the Botswana channel had now been stretched to its limit until railways had been built, and in the meantime, as a result of Livingstone's journeys of 1853–56 and 1858–64, a second line of advance, northwestwards up the Zambezi and Shire rivers, had been begun. This was pioneered by the missionaries from 1875–76 onwards, but at first was too remote to attract to it the same weight of hunting, trading, and settling activity that had expanded up the first route from the settlement base in the Cape Colony. However, the complications resulting from the conflict between the African Lakes Company and the Arab slave-traders, and from the presence of British missionaries in the hinterland of a Portuguese coastal colony, led eventually to the British protectorate in Nyasaland, and, with the financial backing of Rhodes, to the extension of British rule into the eastern part of what was to become Northern Rhodesia. Here the two lines of advance joined together. Further advance to the north was checked by work of the agents of Leopold II's Congo Free State and by the existence of German East Africa (Map 49).

49   The European Advance into Central and East Africa

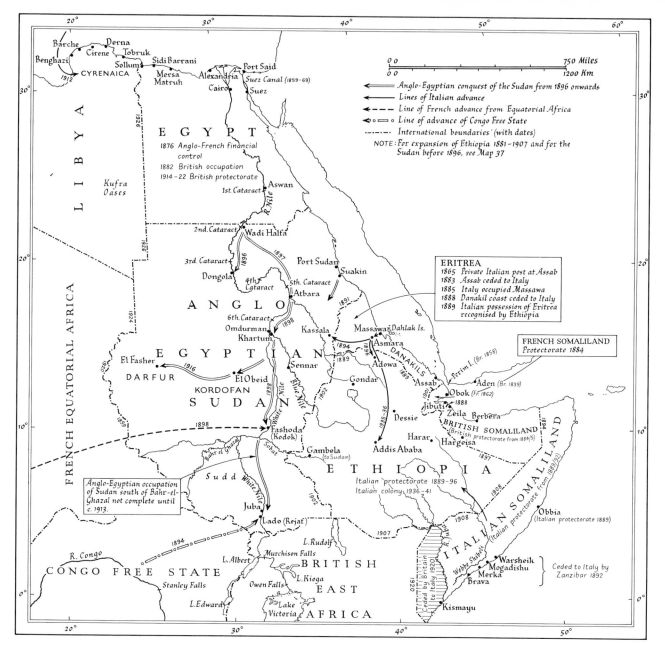

50 The European Advance into North-East Africa

Note: The British occupation of Egypt continued until 1936, when, by the Anglo-Egyptian Treaty of that year, it was limited to the Suez Canal zone. This was not evacuated by the British until after the Treaty of 1954. Egypt remained nominally under Turkish suzerainty until 1914, and was proclaimed a British protectorate in that year only to meet the situation created by the war of 1914–18.

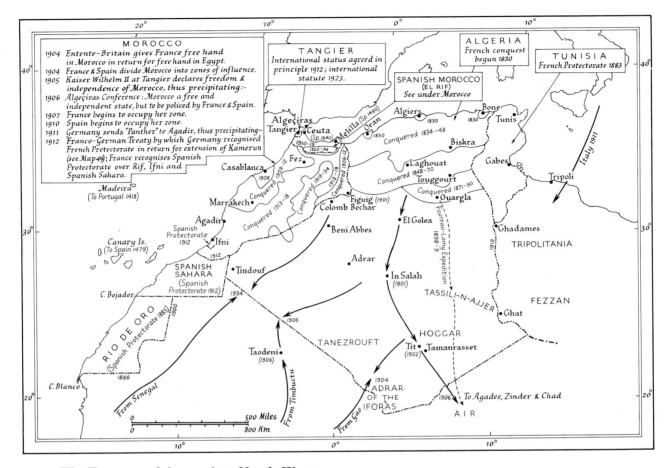

The European Advance into North-West Africa

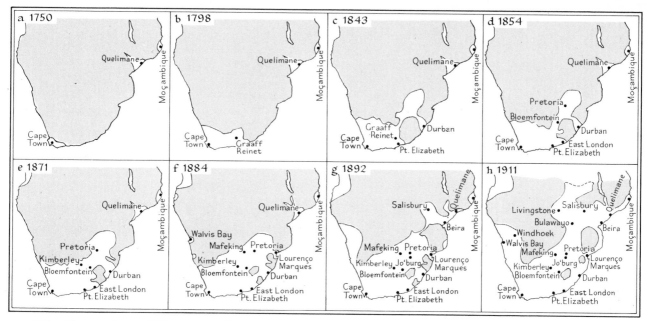

52 The Expansion of European Settlement in Southern Africa

The white areas are intended to indicate the regions dominated by white settlers at the various dates. The frontiers shown between 'white Africa' and 'black Africa' can only be regarded as approximate. In the last sketch, h, there is the additional complication that at this time European settlement was also advancing from the north.

53 to 60 The Pattern of Alien Rule in Africa, 1830–1965

On Maps 53–59, two basic kinds of marking are used throughout for the British territories in Africa to differentiate between those territories directly controlled from Britain (complete shading) and those which enjoyed at least internal self-government (partial shading, round the boundaries only). The latter kind of marking is used for the Cape Colony after it had received self-government in 1872, for Natal after the grant of self-government in 1893, and for the Union of South Africa and for Ghana (the former Gold Coast) after they had achieved dominion status in 1909 and 1957 respectively. It should, however, be noted that the forms of self-government granted to Southern Rhodesia in 1923 and to the Federation of Rhodesia and Nyasaland in 1953 reserved certain powers to the United Kingdom Government, and they have accordingly been treated as though they were wholly dependent territories. Partial shading has also been used for Ethiopia on the map for 1895, the position here being that Ethiopia did not acknowledge the Italian Government's claim that the country was under its protection as a result of the Treaty of Ucciali (1889). With this exception, protectorates have not been distinguished from formal colonies, but broken lines are used throughout to indicate territories held as Mandates of the League of Nations and as Trusteeship territories under the United Nations. On the situation in Egypt between 1882 and 1954, see also the note to Map 50.

A swift revolution swept over political Africa after 1957, when Ghana gained its independence. Map 60 shows the situation in 1965. Colonial status was now a rarity. Thus the remaining colonies are all shown in black, irrespective of their ownership. The independent states are in white, with the dates of their independence given. The shaded territories are those whose status in 1965 was transitional.

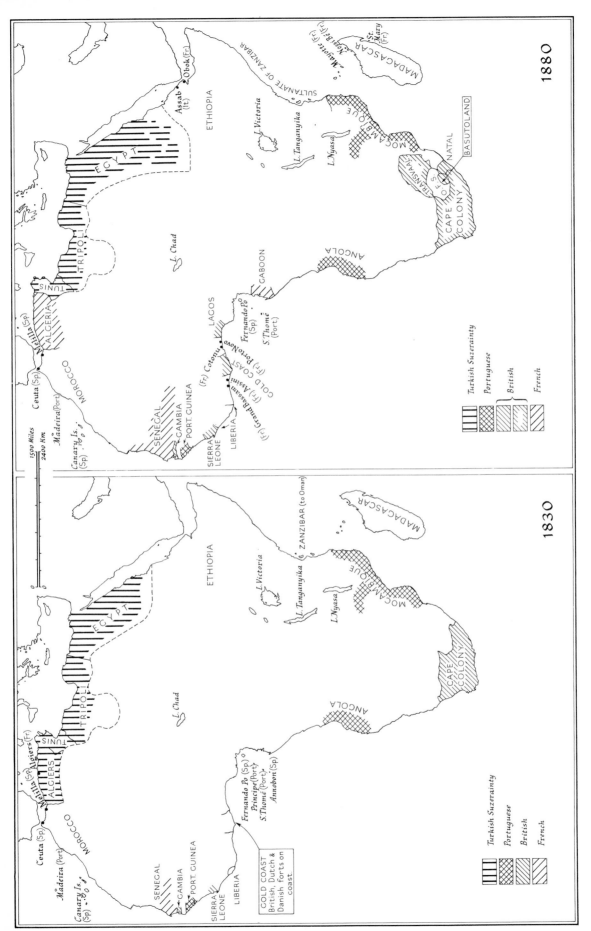

53   The Pattern of Alien Rule in Africa, 1830

54   The Pattern of Alien Rule in Africa, 1880

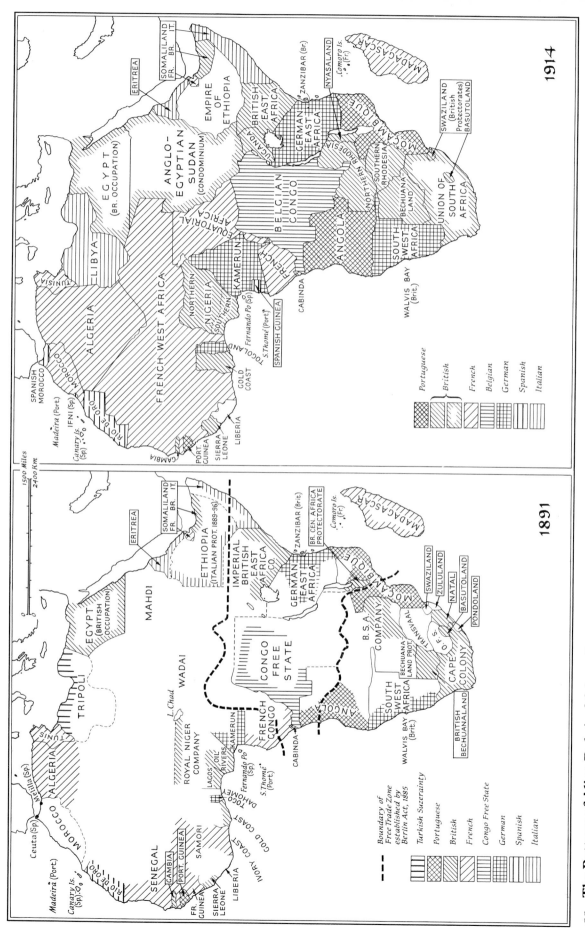

55 The Pattern of Alien Rule in Africa, 1891

56 The Pattern of Alien Rule in Africa, 1914

57 The Pattern of Alien Rule in Africa, 1924

58 The Pattern of Alien Rule in Africa, 1939

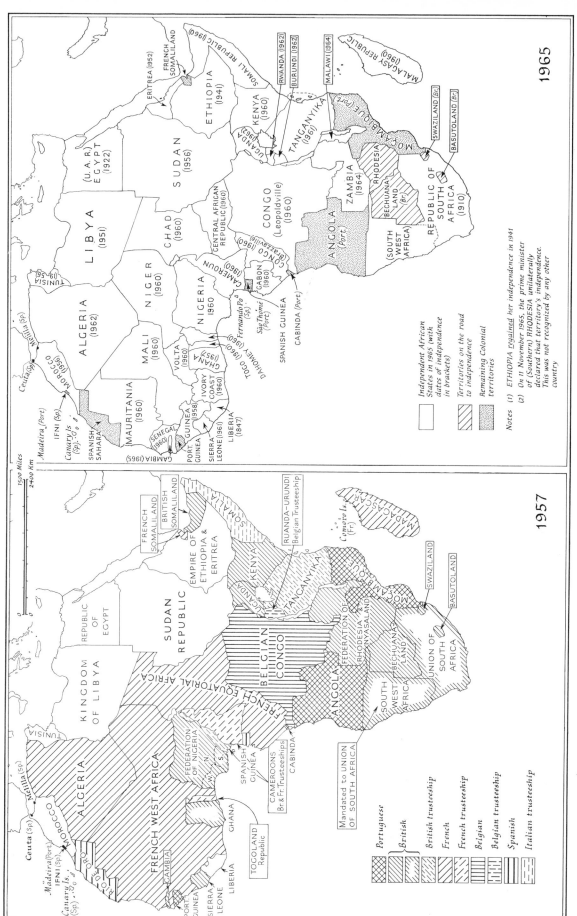

1965

ERITREA (1952)
FRENCH SOMALILAND (1960)
SOMALI REPUBLIC (1960)
ETHIOPIA (1941)
KENYA (1960)
UGANDA (1962)
RWANDA (1962)
BURUNDI (1962)
MALAWI (1964)
TANGANYIKA (1961)
MALAGASY REPUBLIC (1960)
MOZAMBIQUE (Port.)
SWAZILAND (Br.)
BASUTOLAND (Br.)
(U.A.R.) EGYPT (1922)
SUDAN (1956)
CENTRAL AFRICAN REPUBLIC (1960)
CONGO (Leopoldville) (1960)
ZAMBIA (1964)
RHODESIA
BECHUANA-LAND (Br.)
REPUBLIC OF SOUTH AFRICA (1910)
(SOUTH WEST AFRICA)
ANGOLA (Port.)
LIBYA (1951)
CHAD (1960)
NIGER (1960)
CONGO (Brazzaville) (1960)
CAMEROUN (1960)
GABON (1960)
CABINDA (Port.)
SPANISH GUINEA
São Thomé (Port.)
Fernando Po (Sp.)
TUNISIA (1956)
ALGERIA (1962)
MALI (1960)
NIGERIA 1960
VOLTA (1960)
GHANA (1957)
TOGO (1960)
DAHOMEY (1960)
IVORY COAST (1960)
Melilla (Sp.)
Ceuta (Sp.)
MOROCCO (1956)
Madeira (Port.)
IFNI (Sp.)
Canary Is. (Sp.)
SPANISH SAHARA
MAURITANIA (1960)
SENEGAL (1960)
PORT. GUINEA
GUINEA (1958)
SIERRA LEONE (1961)
LIBERIA (1847)
GAMBIA (1965)

Independent African States in 1965 (with dates of independence in brackets)

Territories on the road to independence

Remaining Colonial territories

Notes (1) ETHIOPIA regained her independence in 1941
(2) On 11 November 1965, the prime minister of (Southern) RHODESIA unilaterally declared that territory's independence. This was not recognized by any other country

1957

FRENCH SOMALILAND
BRITISH SOMALILAND
EMPIRE OF ETHIOPIA & ERITREA
SOMALILAND
RUANDA–URUNDI Belgian Trusteeship
Comoro Is. (Fr.)
MADAGASCAR
REPUBLIC OF EGYPT
SUDAN REPUBLIC
KINGDOM OF LIBYA
FRENCH EQUATORIAL AFRICA
BELGIAN CONGO
UGANDA
KENYA
TANGANYIKA
ZANZIBAR
SWAZILAND
BASUTOLAND
FEDERATION OF RHODESIA & NYASALAND
BECHUANA-LAND
UNION OF SOUTH AFRICA
SOUTH WEST AFRICA
Mandated to UNION OF SOUTH AFRICA
ANGOLA
TUNISIA
ALGERIA
MOROCCO
Ceuta (Sp.)
Melilla (Sp.)
Madeira (Port.)
IFNI (Sp.)
Canary Is. (Sp.)
FRENCH WEST AFRICA
FEDERATION OF NIGERIA
N.W.N.
S.
SPANISH GUINEA
CAMEROONS Br & Fr Trusteeships
CABINDA
GAMBIA
GHANA
TOGOLAND Republic
PORT. GUINEA
SIERRA LEONE
LIBERIA

1500 Miles
2400 Km

Portuguese
British
British trusteeship
French
French trusteeship
Belgian
Belgian trusteeship
Spanish
Italian trusteeship

59   **The Pattern of Alien Rule in Africa, 1957**

60   **The Pattern of Alien Rule in Africa, 1965: the Rise of Independent States**

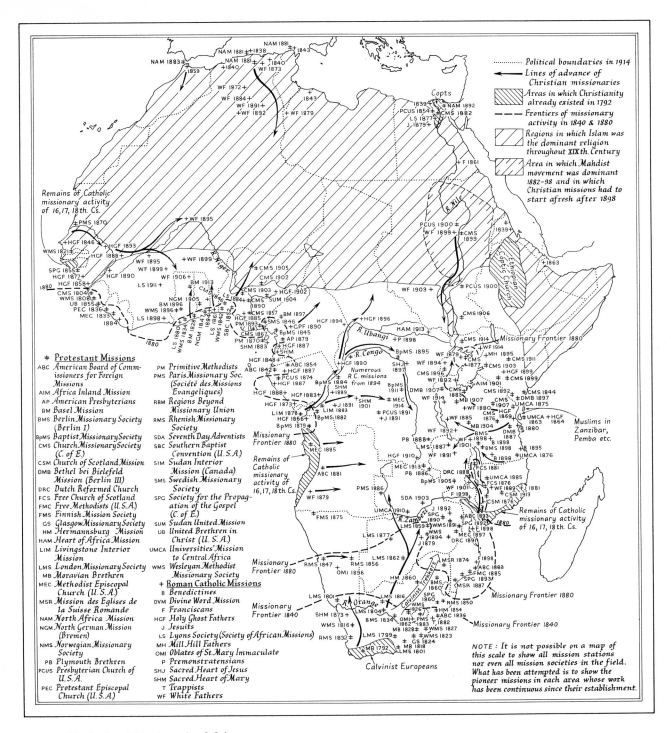

61 Christian Missions in Africa, 1792–1914

Notice how, following in the wake of the explorers, the missionary pioneers made good use of the natural channels of communication into the interior presented by the major waterways, in particular the Congo, the Zambezi and Shire and the East African lakes, and the Senegal and upper Niger.

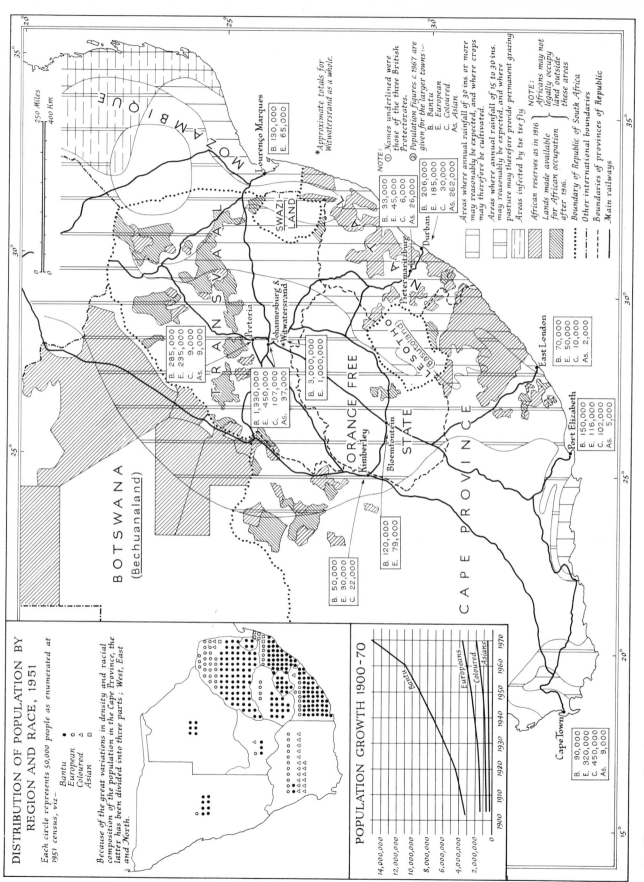

62 European Settlement in South Africa

Some of the information contained in this map is based on maps which appear in *Southern Africa, a geographical study*, by J. H. Wellington, by kind permission of the Syndics of Cambridge University Press.

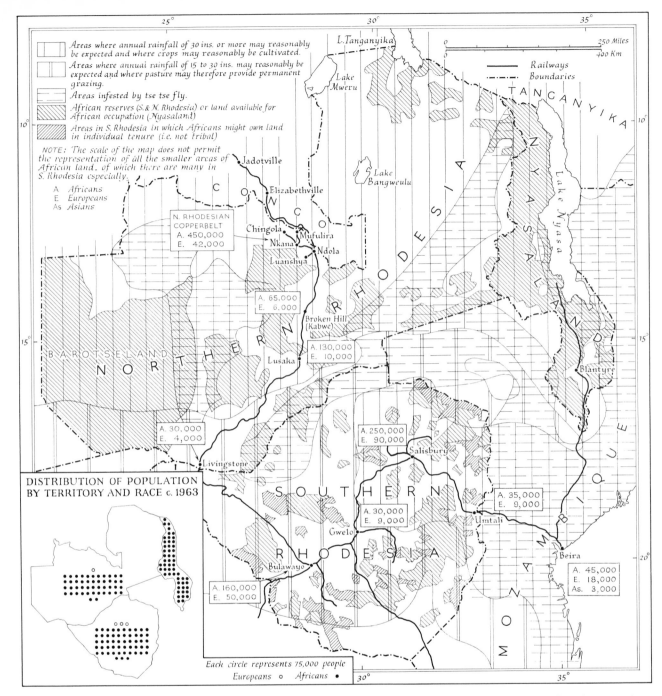

Areas where annual rainfall of 30 ins. or more may reasonably be expected and where crops may reasonably be cultivated.

Areas where annual rainfall of 15 to 30 ins. may reasonably be expected and where pasture may therefore provide permanent grazing.

Areas infested by tse tse fly.

African reserves (S.& N. Rhodesia) or land available for African occupation (Nyasaland)

Areas in S. Rhodesia in which Africans might own land in individual tenure (i.e. not tribal)

NOTE: The scale of the map does not permit the representation of all the smaller areas of African land, of which there are many in S. Rhodesia especially.

A Africans
E Europeans
As Asians

N. RHODESIAN COPPERBELT
A. 450,000
E. 42,000

A. 65,000
E. 6,000

A. 130,000
E. 10,000

A. 30,000
E. 4,000

A. 250,000
E. 90,000

A. 35,000
E. 9,000

A. 30,000
E. 9,000

A. 45,000
E. 18,000
As. 3,000

A. 160,000
E. 50,000

Railways
Boundaries

250 Miles
400 Km

L. Tanganyika
Lake Mweru
Lake Bangweulu
Lake Nyasa

TANGANYIKA
NORTHERN RHODESIA
NYASALAND
SOUTHERN RHODESIA
MOZAMBIQUE
BAROTSELAND
CONGO

Jadotville
Elizabethville
Chingola
Nkana
Mufulira
Ndola
Luanshya
Broken Hill (Kabwe)
Lusaka
Blantyre
Salisbury
Umtali
Beira
Gwelo
Bulawayo
Livingstone

DISTRIBUTION OF POPULATION BY TERRITORY AND RACE c.1963

Each circle represents 75,000 people
Europeans o   Africans •

63 European Settlement in Central Africa, c.1960

Some of the information contained in this map is based on maps which appear in the Report of the Rhodesia–Nyasaland Commission (Cmd. 5949) by kind permission of the Controller of H.M. Stationery Office; and in *Southern Africa, a geographical study*, by J. H. Wellington, by kind permission of the Syndics of Cambridge University Press.

62–5 Maps Showing European Settlement in Africa

Note that, whereas on maps 62 and 63 it is *land available for native African occupation* that is shown by close shading, on maps 64 and 65 the convention is reversed and the close shading indicates *land occupied by or alienated to Europeans.*

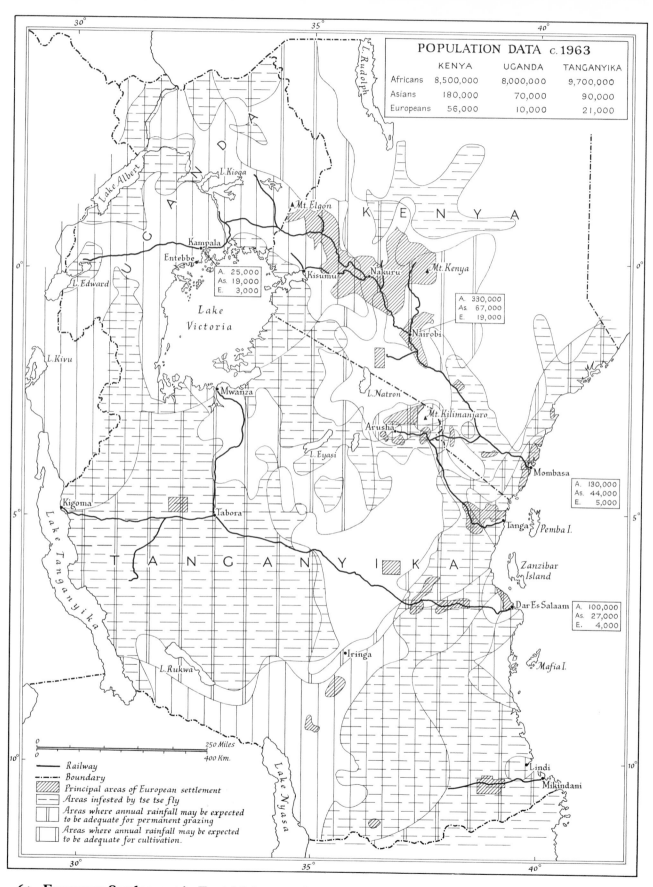

POPULATION DATA c. 1963

	KENYA	UGANDA	TANGANYIKA
Africans	8,500,000	8,000,000	9,700,000
Asians	180,000	70,000	90,000
Europeans	56,000	10,000	21,000

L.Rudolph

U G A N D A

K E N Y A

L.Kioga

▲Mt.Elgon

Kampala

Entebbe
A. 25,000
As. 19,000
E. 3,000

L.Edward

Kisumu

Nakuru

▲Mt.Kenya

Lake
Victoria

A. 330,000
As. 67,000
E. 19,000

Nairobi

L.Kivu

Mwanza

L.Natron

▲Mt.Kilimanjaro

Arusha

L.Eyasi

Mombasa

A. 130,000
As. 44,000
E. 5,000

Kigoma

Tabora

Tanga // Pemba I.

Lake Tanganyika

T A N G A N Y I K A

Zanzibar
Island

Dar Es Salaam

A. 100,000
As. 27,000
E. 4,000

•Iringa

Mafia I.

L.Rukwa

0   250 Miles
0   400 Km.

—— Railway
—·— Boundary

Principal areas of European settlement
Areas infested by tse tse fly
Areas where annual rainfall may be expected
to be adequate for permanent grazing
Areas where annual rainfall may be expected
to be adequate for cultivation

Lake Nyasa

Lindi

Mikindani

64 European Settlement in East Africa, *c.*1963

Some of the information in this map is based on maps contained in
the Report of the East Africa Royal Commission, 1953–55 (Cmd.
9475) by kind permission of the Controller of H.M. Stationery
Office.

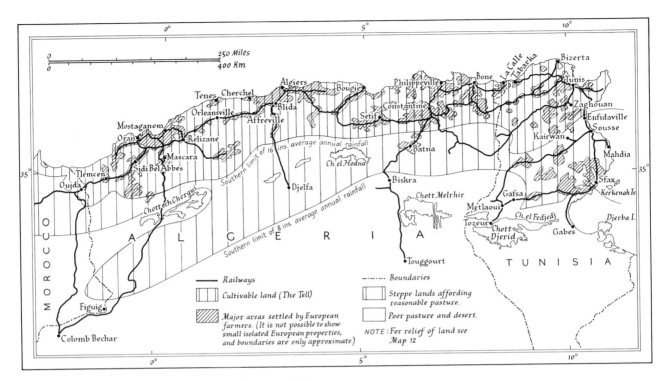

65 European Settlement in North Africa, c. 1950

Morocco is not included in the map, partly because European settlement there on any scale began much later than was the case in Algeria and Tunisia, but chiefly because it is predominantly urban rather than rural.

Approximate populations	Muslims	Jews	Europeans	Total
Tunisia (1946)	2,830,000	70,000	240,000	3,140,000
Algeria (1954)	8,350,000	150,000	1,000,000	9,500,000
Morocco:				
French (1954)	7,700,000	200,000	440,000	8,340,000
Spanish (1950)	917,000	8,000	85,000	1,010,000
Tangier (1953)	105,000	15,000	40,000	160,000

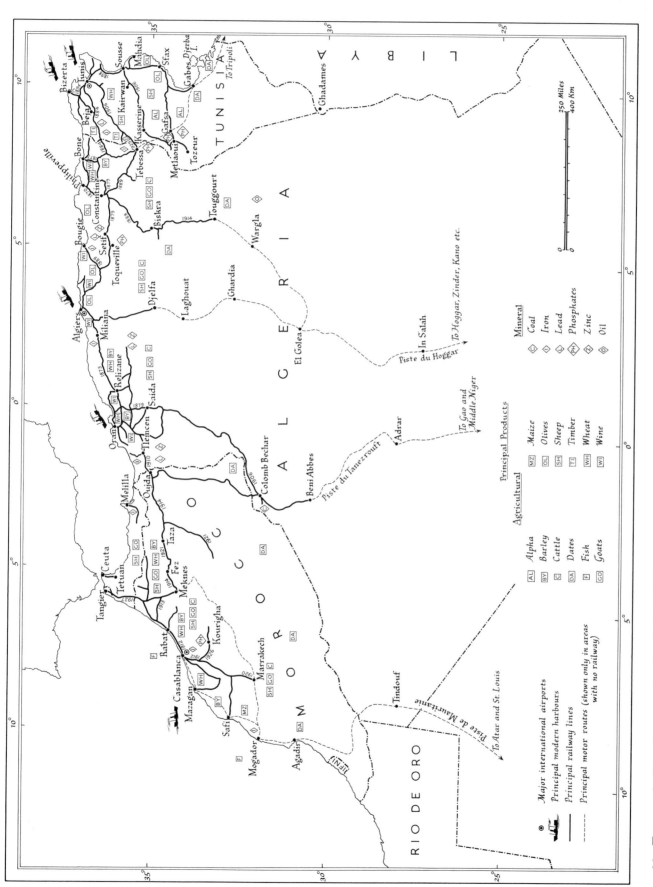

66 Economic Development in the Colonial Period, North-West Africa

It is impossible to show all the numerous small rivers of this area of Africa, but it must be remembered that, although they are of no navigational value, extensive use of them has been made through dams creating reservoirs for purposes of irrigation and hydro-electric power. Another fact not revealed by the map is that most of the large towns had a fair amount of secondary industry.

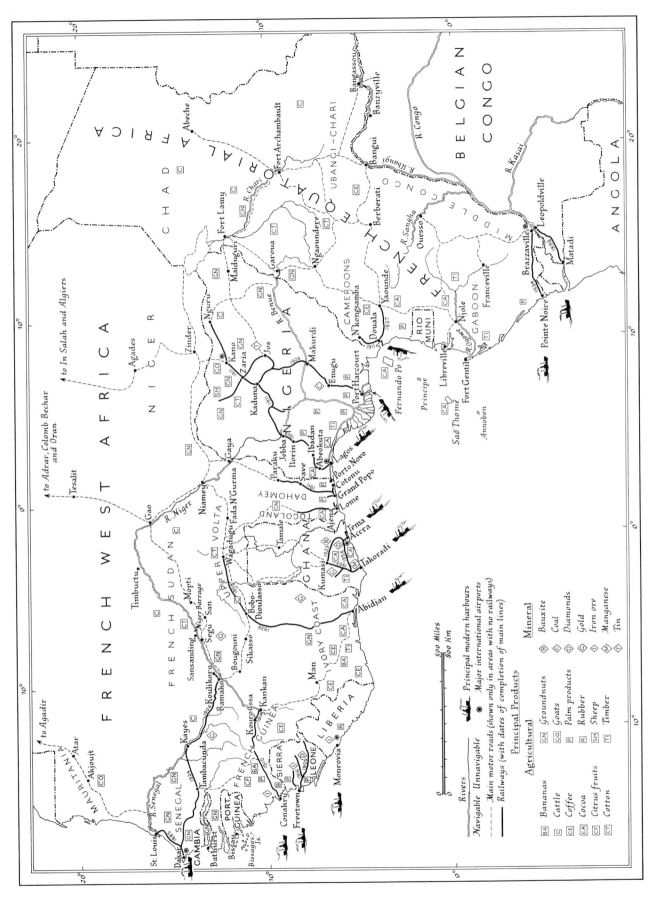

67 Economic Development in the Colonial Period, North-West Africa

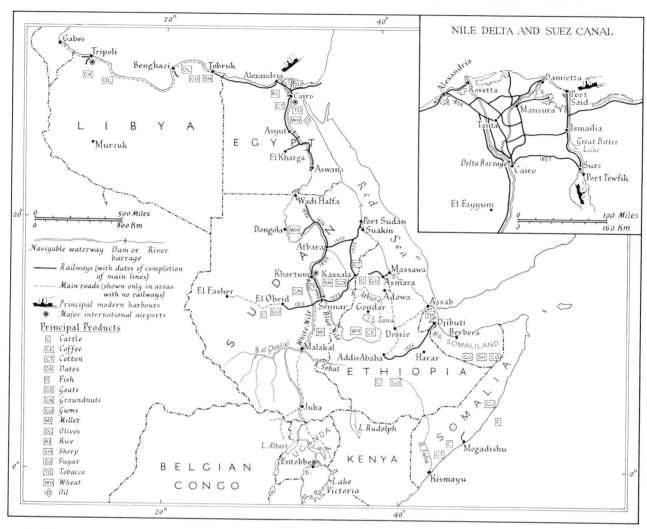

NILE DELTA AND SUEZ CANAL

Alexandria
Rosetta
1856
Damietta
Port Said
Mansura
Tanta
Ismailia
Delta Barrage
Cairo
1857
Great Bitter Lake
El Fayyum
Suez
Port Tewfik

0   100 Miles
0   160 Km

Gabes
Tripoli
DA
CO
Benghazi
OL
Tobruk
SH
Alexandria
CT
SU

L I B Y A
Murzuk

RI
Cairo
CT
TO
WH
Asyut
El Kharga
Aswan

E G Y P T

Red Sea

Wadi Halfa
Dongola
WH
S U D A N
Atbara
1906
Port Sudan
Suakin

Khartum
Kassala
CT
CT
SH
CO
C
GU
Massawa
Asmara
Adowa
Adowa
Assab

El Fasher
GN
El Obeid
C
GU
1912
Sennar
R. Atbara
Gondar
L. Tana
WH
CE
Dessie
SH
Djibuti
Berbera
BR
SOMALILAND
GU
SH
CO

B. el Ghazal
White Nile
Blue Nile
MI
Malakal
AddisAbaba
1926
Harar
C
GU

R. Sobat
E T H I O P I A
C
GU
GU

Juba
L. Rudolph
S O M A L I A
F

L. Albert
UGANDA
KENYA
CT
Mogadishu

Entebbe
Lake Victoria
R. Juba
C
Kismayu

BELGIAN CONGO

Navigable waterway   Dam or River barrage
——— Railways (with dates of completion of main lines)
- - - Main roads (shown only in areas with no railways)
Principal modern harbours
Major international airports

Principal Products
C   Cattle
CE   Coffee
CT   Cotton
DA   Dates
F   Fish
GO   Goats
GN   Groundnuts
GU   Gums
MI   Millet
OL   Olives
RI   Rice
SH   Sheep
SU   Sugar
TO   Tobacco
WH   Wheat
◇   Oil

0   500 Miles
0   800 Km

68   Economic Development to c.1960, North-East Africa

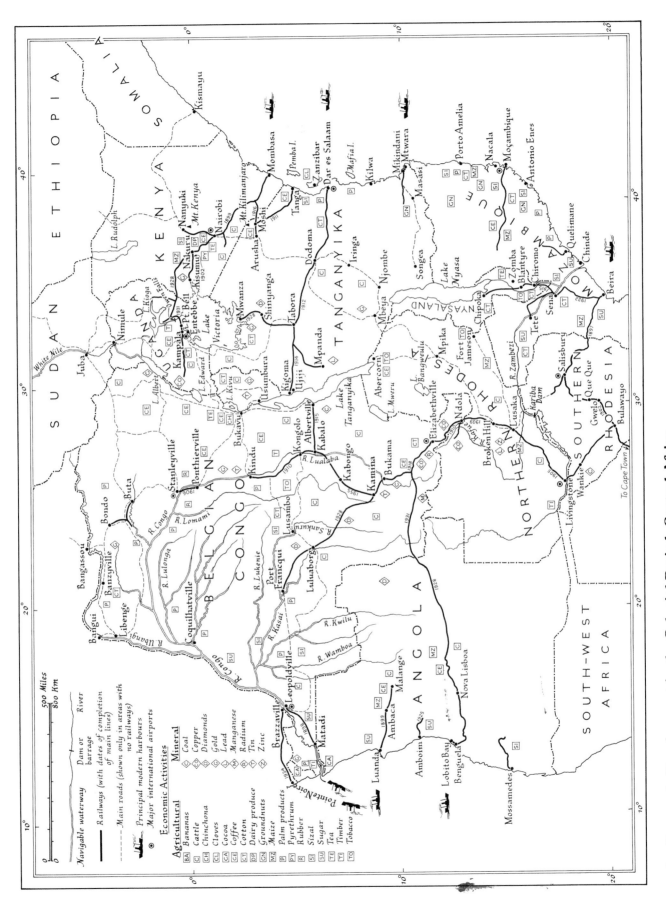

69 Economic Development in the Colonial Period, Central Africa

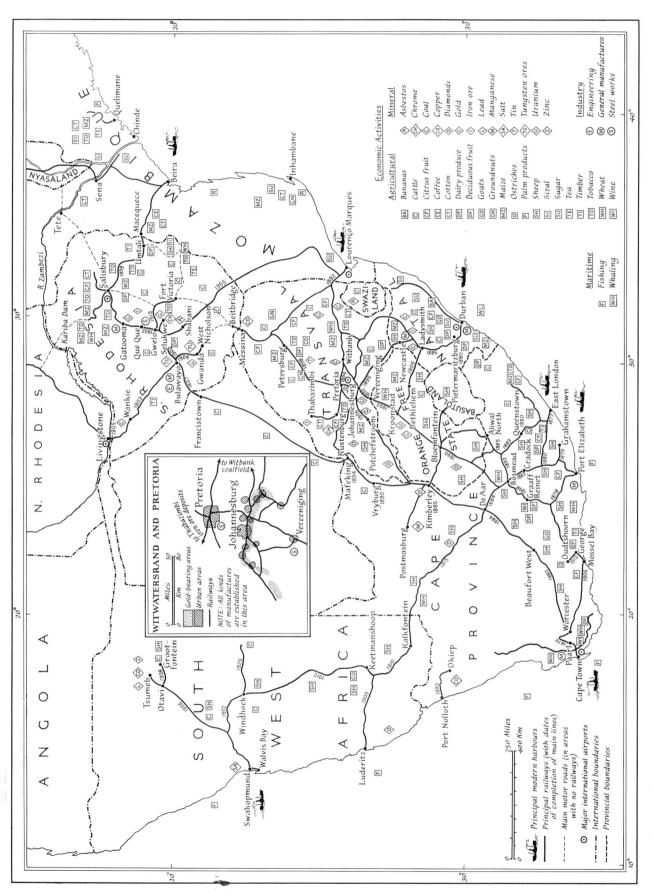

70 Economic Development to c.1960, South Africa

Rivers are not shown on this map. The rivers of South Africa are of no use for navigation and are not very suitable for dams for purposes of irrigation and the production of hydro-electric power, since they are generally shallow and suffer from great seasonal variations in their flow.

Economic Activities

Agricultural

Bananas	BA
Cattle	C
Citrus fruit	CF
Coffee	CE
Cotton	CO
Dairy produce	DP
Deciduous fruit	DF
Goats	G
Groundnuts	GO
Maize	MZ
Ostriches	O
Palm products	P
Sheep	SH
Sizal	SI
Sugar	SU
Tea	TE
Timber	TI
Tobacco	TO
Wheat	WH
Wine	WI

Mineral

Asbestos	A
Chrome	SH
Coal	CO
Copper	CO
Diamonds	◇
Gold	◇
Iron ore	◇
Lead	◇
Manganese	MN
Salt	SA
Tin	T
Tungsten ores	TU
Uranium	◇
Zinc	Z

Industry

Engineering	E
General manufactures	M
Steel works	S

Maritime

Fishing	F
Whaling	WH

Key

- Principal modern harbours
- Principal railways (with dates of completion of main lines)
- Main motor roads (in areas with no railways)
- ⊙ Major international airports
- International boundaries
- Provincial boundaries

Scale: 250 Miles / 400 Km

WITWATERSRAND AND PRETORIA

Scale: 0 50 80 Miles / Km

- Gold-bearing areas
- Urban areas
- Railways

NOTE: All kinds of manufactures are established in this area

to Witbank coalfield
to Thabazimbi iron ore deposits
Pretoria
Johannesburg
Vereeniging

71 Independent Africa, 1976

This map should be compared with Map 60, The Pattern of Alien Rule in Africa, 1965. Only dates of independence occurring after 1965 are shown on this map.

Appendix: Some Post Colonial Name Changes

Colonial Name	Modern African Name	Colonial Name	Modern African Name
Algeria		Chad (Tchad)	
Bone	Annaba	Fort-Lamy	Ndjamena
Bougie	Bejaia		
Colomb-Béchar	Bechar		
Fort Polignac	Illizi		
Orléansville	El Asnam		
Philippeville	Skika	Dahomey	Republic of Bénin
Anglo-Egyptian Sudan	Democratic Republic of the Sudan	Eritrea	part of Ethiopia
		French Congo (Moyen Congo	People's Republic of the Congo (Congo Brazzaville)
Basutoland	Lesotho		
Bechuanaland	Botswana		
Gaberones	Gaborone		
		French Guinea (Guinée)	Republic of Guinea (Guinée)
Belgian Congo	Zaire		
Léopoldville	Kinshasha		
Bakwanga	Mbuji-Mayi		
Coquilhatville	Mbandaka		
Costermansville	Bukavu	French Sudan	Mali
Elizabethville	Lubumbashi		
Jadotville	Likasi		
Luluabourg	Kananga		
Stanleyville	Kisangani		
Stanley Pool	Malebo Pool	French Togoland	Togo (Togolese Republic)
British Somaliland	part of Somali Democratic Republic (Somalia)		
		Gambia	The Gambia
		Bathurst	Banjul
Cameroons	Cameroun	Gold Coast	Ghana

Colonial Name	Modern African Name	Colonial Name	Modern African Name

Italian Somaliland	part of Somali Democratic Republic (Somalia)	Ruanda
		  Astrida
		  Shangugu
			Rwanda
			  Butare
			  Cyangugu

Madagascar	Malagasy Republic (République Malgache)	Southern Rhodesia	(Zimbabwe)
		South-West Africa	Namibia

Mauritania
  Port Etienne
  Fort Gouraud
	Islamic Republic of Mauritania
	  Nouadhibou
	  Fderik
		Spanish Guinea
		  Fernando Po
			Equatorial Guinea
			  Macias Nguema Biyogo

Morocco
  Fedala
  Mazagan
  Mogador
  Port Lyautey
	
	Mohammedia
	El-Jadida
	Essaouira
	Kenitra
		Spanish Sahara	shared between Morocco and Mauritania

Mozambique (Moçambique) Lourenço-Marques	 Maputo	Villa Cisneros	Dakhla

Northern Rhodesia
  Abercorn
  Broken Hill
  Fort Jameson
  Fort Roseberg
	Zambia
	  Mbala
	  Kabwe
	  Chipata
	  Mansa
		Tanganyika	joined with Zanzibar in United Republic of Tanzania

		Urundi
		  Usumbura
			Burundi
			  Bujumbura

Oubangui-Chari	Central African Empire		
		Zanzibar	joined with Tanganyika in United Republic of Tanzania
Portuguese Guinea	Guinee-Bissao		

Index of Proper Names

References throughout are to map numbers

Names of geographical features and of places are printed thus: Abay R.; Abeokuta.

Names of countries, provinces, regions, etc., are printed thus: ADRAR; ALGERIA.

Names of individual persons are printed thus: *Abu Yazid*; *Andersson, Charles*.

Names of peoples, associations of persons, languages, etc., are printed thus: *ADANGME*; *ABD AL-WAHIDS*; *AFRICAN LAKES Co.*

Bantu and Arabic names are indexed under the initial letter of their root or substantive name, the Bantu prefix or the Arabic article being shown first without a capital initial. An exception to this rule is where the prefix or article is accepted as part of a geographical name in common usage, unless in the case of Bantu names, it is necessary to show both the 'tribal' and 'location' forms.

Examples:

(1) al-Fustat (under F), but El Fasher (under E);

(2) *wa-CHAGGA* (under *C*), the Chagga people, but MASHONALAND (under M), the land of the *ma-SHONA*.

(3) *ba-GANDA* (people) and bu-GANDA (country of the *ba-GANDA*), both indexed under G.

It should also be noted that the spellings used for African proper names tend to vary between European languages. Thus, for example, in French 'ou' might be found where English has either 'w' or 'u' (e.g. Ouagadougou/Wagadugu), while 'dj' often occurs where English would have 'j' (e.g. Djenne/Jenne).

Abbreviations:

B.	bay
C.	cape
I., Is.	isle, island; isles, islands
L.	lake
Mt., Mts.	mount, mountain; mountains
O.	oasis
R.	river
S., St.	São, Saint, Sainte, etc.

Ortelius's map of Africa, from *Ortelius Theatrum Orbis Terrarum,* published in Antwerp, 1574. Reproduced by courtesy of the British Library Board.